I0815470

Towards a Nude Architecture 裸の建築

Towards a Nude Architecture
裸の建築

Yuval Zohar

A Visual Compendium of Japanese Hot Springs

nai010 publishers

KIRIN

The Springs

As one of the most volcanically active geographies on the globe, Japan gushes with nearly 30,000 naturally occurring hot springs of varying temperatures, colors, and mineral compositions. A literal treasure island: if you dig deep enough, you will strike gold – or emerald-green, cloudy white, bright blue, earthen-red, and bubbling black waters.

The country is filled with an incredible variety of structures designed around these tapped subterranean veins, known as 'onsen' (温泉), along with their public bathhouse counterparts 'sento' (銭湯); from rustic thatched-roof cottages dotted around scalding sulfuric cauldrons, to ocean-side rock outcroppings accessible only at low-tide, verdant forests filled with vernacular soaks, and pristine baths of manicured modernity. These temples to steam and sweat – whose roots can be traced back to the earliest recorded history of ritual cleansing in Buddhism – have served as healing oases in times of war and peace, stood their ground against dogged attacks by moralizing foreign influences, and nursed the country through natural and man-made disasters to become indispensable pillars of contemporary culture. Communal bathing has managed to thrive in spite of, and at times because of, the country's turbulent history, but now finds itself in a precarious position where it must adapt for survival in a new age.

Paying titular homage to the bible of modern architecture written by Le Corbusier, and combining my photos, drawings, collages, and diagrams from over a decade of travel across the country, *Towards a Nude Architecture*

1 Tsurunoyu in Beppu.

is a deep dive into the fascinating world of onsen viewed through an architectural lens. Across three chapters covering past, present, and future, the book looks at the spiritual and medicinal roots of bathing, the range of buildings dedicated to the activity, and a proposed recontextualization in a far-off land.

The Japanese title 'hadaka no kenchiku' (裸の建築), or literally 'naked architecture,' is inspired by the concept of 'hadaka no tsuki ai' (裸の付き合い), which translates into 'naked friendship' and describes the unspoken bond formed at the dissolution of social hierarchies as both clothing and status are removed when immersing in the waters of a public bath.

By examining these topics under a microscope and within a viewfinder, the book seeks to discover the base ingredients that combine to make Japanese bathing culture into such a singular experience, showcasing the stylistically bare architecture of onsen which dignifiedly performs its duty, free of frills, as naked as the people it serves. The graphically diverse content presents a visual journey spanning centuries and geographies to convey the enduring impressions of this poetic mingling between architecture, nature, and the human body.

44 Kawarage Oyutaki Falls in Akita.
45 Koganeyu Sento in Tokyo.
54–55 Hoshi Onsen Chojukan in Gunma.
56–57 White Monkey Bath in Fujisan Ryokan.

1 PAST
過去

The History

The story of Japan can be told through water and steam. So closely does the history of hot springs project onto the country's national identity, that the circle on the flag could represent a bath in plan view. Enjoyed across species and cultures from antiquity through the current era, it is uniquely in Japan where, almost as a reward for the remarkably volatile landscape, onsen have achieved such profound status.

Public bathing in the modern Japanese context started very differently from how we know it today. While onsen in the wild have been used for thousands of years in purification rituals of religious ceremonies, then as hidden bases for recuperating samurai, and later as testbeds for pioneering medical advances, the first public bathhouses were originally steam-based. Known as mushiburo (蒸し風呂), these sauna-like rooms gradually gave way to the iconic water-filled tubs of the modern-day Japanese sento. The narrative of how this cultural relic not only endured, but flourished in the presence of great challenges has been passed through folkloric legends, battle chronicles, moving poetry, and dynamic woodblock prints splashed throughout the country's tempestuous history.

Baths in Japan range in scale from single-bather barrels to 'one-thousand person baths' (senninburo 千人風呂) and vary wildly in type: indoor baths (uchiburo 内風呂), outdoor baths (rotenburo 露天風呂), male baths (otokoyu 男湯), female baths (onnayu 女湯) mixed-gender baths (konyoku 混浴), large communal baths (daiyokujo 大浴場), private baths (kashikiriburo 貸切風呂), foot baths (ashiyu 足湯), hand baths

1 Tamagawa Onsen in Akita, fed by Japan's single most productive hot spring source.

(teyu 手湯), waterfall baths (utaseyu 打たせ湯), sand baths (sunaburo 砂風呂), mud baths (doroyu 泥湯), hot stone baths (ganbanyoku 岩盤浴), cave baths (gankutsuburo 岩窟風呂), sleeping baths (neyu 寝湯), sitting baths (suwariyu 座り湯), standing baths (tachiyu 立ち湯), walking baths (hokofuro 歩行風呂), jet baths (jetto basu ジェットバス), medicinal baths (kusuriyu 薬湯), electric baths (denkiburo 電気風呂), cold baths (mizuburo 水風呂), and more can all be encountered around the country, each with their own unique geological fingerprint represented in their mineral composition.

Bathing has even made its way onto the national calendar. The number two can be shortened to 'fu' (from futatsu 二つ, meaning two of something) and six condensed to 'ro' (from 'roku' 六, the number six), when put together these make 'furo,' the Japanese word for bath. November 26 is 'Good Bath Day' because 11 can be read as 'ii' (いい) meaning 'good,' and June 26 is 'Outdoor Bath Day' as it sounds like the shortening of 'rotenburo.'

With such deep societal roots, it might be surprising, then, that the future of onsen and sento is uncertain. As quaint neighborhood soaks are continually replaced by individual home baths or colossal 'super sento,' public bathing culture is eroding to both extremes of the scale, reaching an inflection point that deserves critical investigation. Facing declining visitors and increased privatization, compounded by recent global crises, the need to promote and preserve these bastions of public space has never been more crucial.

3

THE SOURCE

How onsen come into being is a complex process involving largely invisible subterranean mechanisms, as the earth itself becomes a giant boiler, imbuing water with special properties.

Onsen water is classified into volcanic and non-volcanic. Volcanic hot springs arise from rainwater or snow that has seeped into the ground which, following roughly 50 years of heating from volcanic gasses and magma, finally emerges as searing mineral springs. Non-volcanic water is further separated into deep groundwater, which is heated geothermally by elevated underground temperatures, and fossilized seawater, which is trapped by movements in the earth's crust. The water then erupts, gushes, or is drilled to the surface to be contained and enjoyed.

2 Sulfur crystal formation in Tamagawa Onsen Nature Research Path.
3 Acidic waters fed from the nearby Obuki Spring form a river.

Black 黒 White 白

Blue 青 Green 緑

Orange 橙 Yellow 黄

THE COLORS

Onsen have a diverse range of color, temperature, pH, smell, taste, and texture, with quality varying greatly depending on how and where they are formed. The green/blue acidic waters of Kusatsu Onsen, pictured left, contain sulfur, aluminum sulfate, and chloride. The different hues are not only representative of the distinct terrain of certain regions throughout the country but are, in some cases, valued for their rarity along with the curative effects that they have on the body.

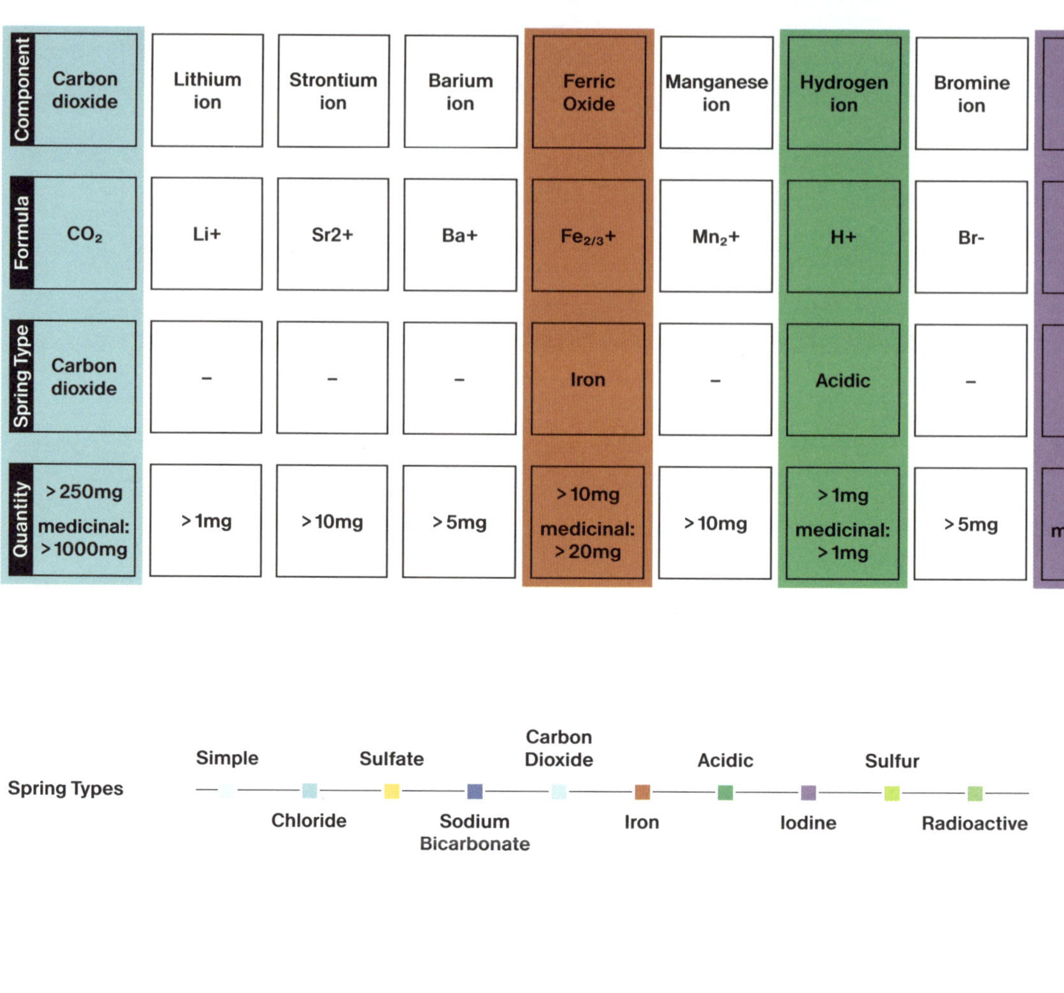

Component	Carbon dioxide	Lithium ion	Strontium ion	Barium ion	Ferric Oxide	Manganese ion	Hydrogen ion	Bromine ion	Iodi io
Formula	CO_2	Li+	Sr2+	Ba+	$Fe_{2/3}$+	Mn_2+	H+	Br-	I-
Spring Type	Carbon dioxide	–	–	–	Iron	–	Acidic	–	Iodi
Quantity	> 250mg medicinal: > 1000mg	> 1mg	> 10mg	> 5mg	> 10mg medicinal: > 20mg	> 10mg	> 1mg medicinal: > 1mg	> 5mg	> 1n medic > 10

pH Scale

Acidic — Neutral — Alkaline

0 — 3 — 6 — 7.5 — 8.5 — 14

Weak Acidic — Weak Alkaline

THE MINERALS

According to the Hot Springs Law enacted in 1948, onsen are defined as water, water vapor, or other gasses that emerge from the earth, either naturally or from artificially bored holes, with a temperature higher than 25°C, or containing at least one of the specified amounts of the minerals in this chart per 1 kg of water. In addition, a body of water will qualify as an onsen if it has 1,000 mg/kg of dissolved substances. The quality of the spring water is determined by elements classified by the Ministry of the Environment in 1978 and updated in 2014 into groups reflecting the main component of each spring: simple (単純温泉), carbon dioxide (二酸化炭素泉), sodium bicarbonate (炭酸水素塩泉), chloride (塩化物泉), iodine (含よう素泉), sulfate (硫酸塩泉), iron (含鉄泉), sulfur (硫黄泉), acidic (酸性泉), and radioactive (放射能泉) springs. The color of each is further determined by light reflection, refraction, absorption, and turbidity.

oride on	Hydrogen Arsenate	Arsenic acid	Sulfur	Metaboric acid	Metasilicic acid	Sodium Bicarbonate	Radon	Radium
-	$HAsO_4$	$HAsO_2$	S	HBO_2	H_2SiO_3	$NaHCO_3$	Ra	Rn
–	–	–	Sulfur	–	–	–	Radioactive	–
mg	> 1.3mg	> 1mg	> 1mg medicinal > 2mg	> 5mg	> 50mg	> 340mg	$>20\times10^{-10}$Ci medicinal $>30\times10^{-10}$Ci	$>10^{-8}$mg

Temperature: Cool — 25°C — Warm — 34°C — Hot — 42°C — Extra hot

Osmotic Pressure: Hypotonic — 8g/kg — Isotonic — 10g/kg — Hypertonic

Although the two classification systems do not directly overlap and springs are often a mix of the categories listed, the chart shows their intersection at a 'therapeutic' designation, one requiring higher amounts of certain minerals. Springs can be further differentiated through their temperature, pH, and osmotic pressure.

The elemental makeup of onsen water is directly correlated with the origin of the source. Volcanoes play a key role in the formation of onsen water, as the mineral content is closely linked to geographical and geological features in which they steep, but geothermal heating and other underground activity can also create onsen water. While there are springs that emerge naturally, drills are often used to bore deep into the ground to retrieve the water and pump it into hot springs facilities.

MUSCULAR

Soaking in a variety of water, including both sulfur and chloride springs, can help alleviate muscle soreness and stiffness.

CARDIOVASCULAR

Several types of water hav been linked to a lower prev alence of hypertension wit regular bathing.

GASTROINTESTINAL

Chloride springs, which can be further categorized as sodium, calcium, and magnesium, are said to improve gastrointestinal issues when ingested, including indigestion, constipation, gas, and a variety of other gastric ailments.

GYNAECOLOGICAL

Other than helping ease menstrual pain, certain hot springs known as 'ferti ity baths,' or kodakaranoyu (子宝の湯), are thought to improve ovarian function based on increased blood activity around the reprodu tive glands.

RHEUMATOLOGICAL

A common source of recuperation through onsen, bathing in the heat of mineral waters reduces pressu on the body, allowing joints to recover in an optimal environment.

DERMAL

Notably, bicarbonate, sulfur, and sulfate springs are known as 'beauty baths' or bijinnoyu (美人の湯), which have rejuvenating effects on the skin and alleviate dermatitis, psoriasis, and eczema.

THE THERAPY

From legends of wounded animals recuperating to recorded history of warlords and their soldiers recovering from injuries, the medicinal benefits of onsen have been widely touted for centuries. Through the research of prominent figures such as Gotō Konzan, a practitioner

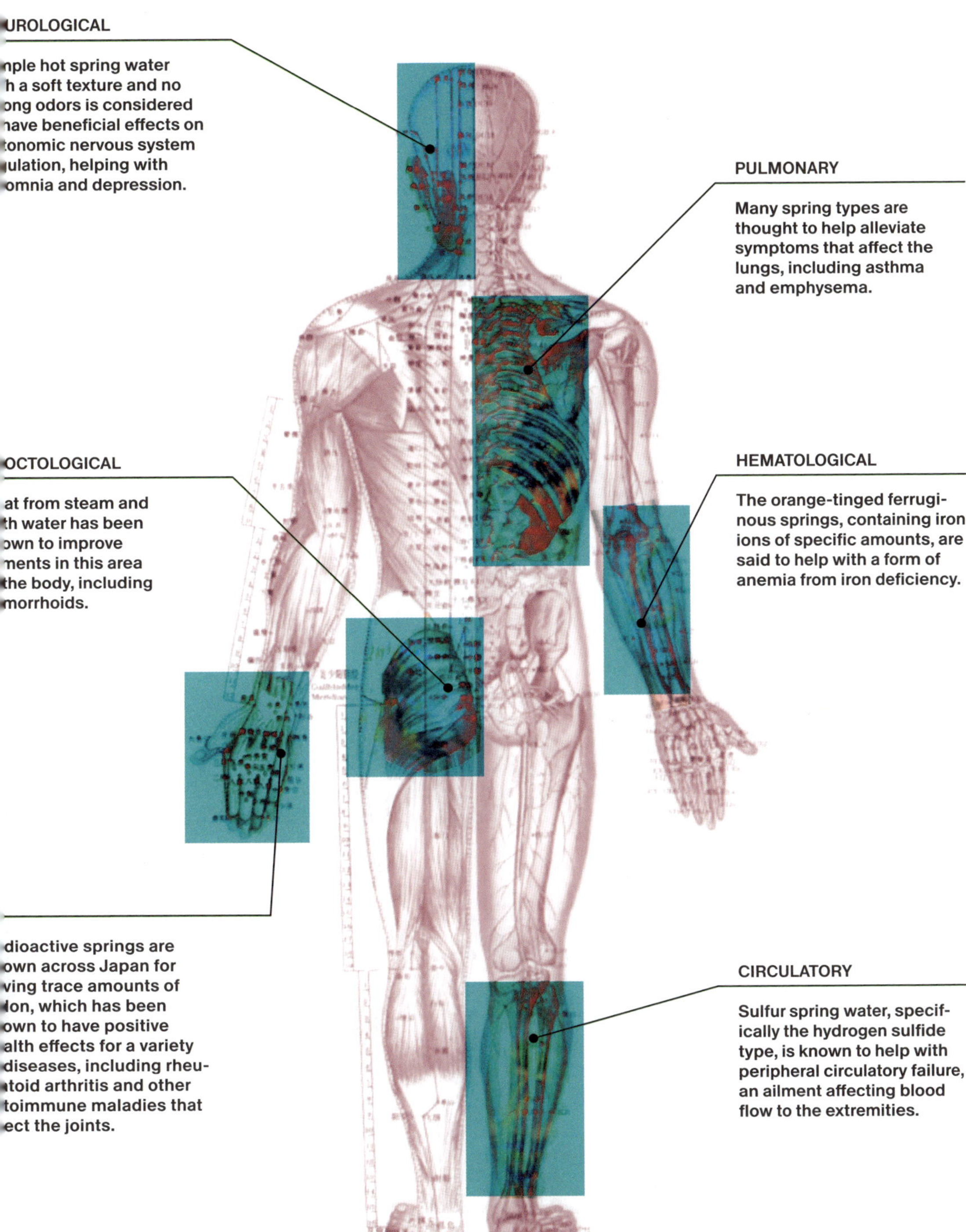

of traditional medicine who led the reformation towards verifiable treatment in Japan, and German Doctor Erwin Bälz, an early proponent of bathing therapy, hot spring treatment or Toji (湯治), which flourished in the Edo period, has now become a full-fledged industry.

4

5

THE FOODS

Onsen tamago (温泉卵), or onsen eggs, are perhaps the best-known hot spring foods. When done right, they achieve some of the best yolk consistency of any cooking method due to the temperatures and minerals unique to the source water.

For centuries, both the boiling water as well as the steam from onsen have been used to cook various delicacies, including vegetables, fruits, tofu, rice, bread, seafood, and meat among others. This culinary technique, known as jigokumushi (地獄蒸し) – literally 'hell steaming' – began in the Edo period and has been carried over through generations as a lasting tradition of meal preparation that utilizes the land itself as a stovetop oven.

4 Fresh eggs are placed in nets and submerged in the sulfurous water of Kuroyu Onsen.
5 The hard-boiled egg shells turn black from the chemical reaction.

6

7

THE DRINKS

Hot spring water offers several benefits when imbibed directly, and in places that offer it straight from the tap, there are specific regulations around how much should be consumed and how to dilute the content if necessary. Onsen water is also used in a variety of beverages, either bottled as mineral-rich water or added to drinks such as cider, beer, and shochu, to enhance the taste, texture, and overall nutritional value of the product. Rarer and usually reserved for special occasions, onsen water can even be used to brew coffee and tea.

6 Onsen water is bottled and sold as a more nutritious version of mineral water.
7 The naturally fizzy springs of Lamune Onsen are added to a cider drink for a perk up.

WHEN SUPERIMPOSED OVER THE HISTORY OF JAPAN, THE TIMELINE OF HOT SPRINGS REVEALS ITSELF AS A COLORFUL THREAD SEWN DEEPLY INTO THE CULTURAL TAPESTRY OF THE COUNTRY, WINDING ITS WAY THROUGH ANCIENT RELIGIONS, WARRING EMPIRES, REINFORCEMENT AND EVENTUAL DECONSTRUCTION OF SOCIAL STRATA, MEDICINAL AND SCIENTIFIC DISCOVERIES, DEVASTATING EARTHQUAKES, A BURGEONING POST-WAR TOURIST INFRASTRUCTURE, AND MODERN-DAY POP CULTURE PASTICHE, INSEPARABLY ENTANGLED. THE HISTORY, PRESENT, AND FUTURE OF BATHING IN JAPAN TELL THE STORY OF THE ISLAND NATION.

PREHISTORIC

300BC–300CE
Prior to the introduction of Buddhism to Japan, it was customary to take a bath when praying to the gods or making a wish, a Shinto practice known as misogi (禊).

297
'The History of the Kingdom of Wei,' a Chinese text, includes the first description of Japanese bathing.

CLASSICAL

552
Buddhism arrives in Japan with ritual bathing both for self-purification and cleansing of the Buddha statue.

672
Emperor Tenmu goes to a kamaburo to recuperate from his battle wounds, these steam baths, along with Iwaburo rock baths, are the oldest types of baths in Japan.

720
Dogo Onsen, along with Shirahama and Arima Onsen, are the earliest recorded hot springs mentioned in 'Nihon Shoki.'

758
In the tradition of Buddhist charity baths called seyoku (施浴), Empress Komyo personally washes a thousand beggars at Horyuji Temple in Nara.

794
Steam baths with medicinal herbs that were the original form of bathing starting in the Nara period give way to the hot-water baths of today.

835

競細腰雪柳風呂
時世粧年中行事之
10
11
13
09
18
24
19
14
03
21
17
12

SENTO ART COLLAGE
A super collage of twenty-five different characters across centuries of sento depictions, ranging from Japanese woodblocks, to western etchings, manga, anime, and video games.

In the Bathhouse
da Koryusai, 1770

02 Onna Yu
Torii Kiyonaga, 1780

03 Washing by Screen
Tamagawa Shucho, 1804

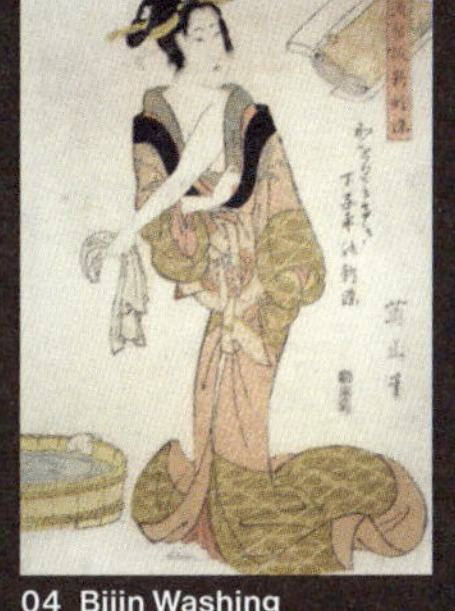

04 Bijin Washing
Kikukawa Eizan, 1820

05 Public Bath at Shimoda
James Fuller, 1856

Aoi
gawa Kunisada, 1857

07 Beauty in Octopus Robe
Utagawa Kunisada, 1858

08 Waterfall Lover
Utagawa Kunisada, 1863

09 Kabuki Actors at Bath
Oju Kunichika Hitsu, 1868

10 Thunder God Bathing
Kubota Beisen, 1894

Interior of Public Bath
gawa Yoshiiku, 19th-c

12 Woman After Bath
Hashiguchi Goyo, 1915

13 Woman at Hot Spring
Hashiguchi Goyo, 1920

14 Woman Washing Face
Hashiguchi Goyo, 1920

15 Woman in Underrobe
Hashiguchi Goyo, 1920

After a Bath
nsen Natori, 1928

17 Woman Combing Hair
Kotondo Torii, 1929

18 Bath Fragrance
Ito Shinsui, 1930

19 Hair
Ito Shinsui, 1953

20 Woman After Bath
Ito Shinsui, 1960

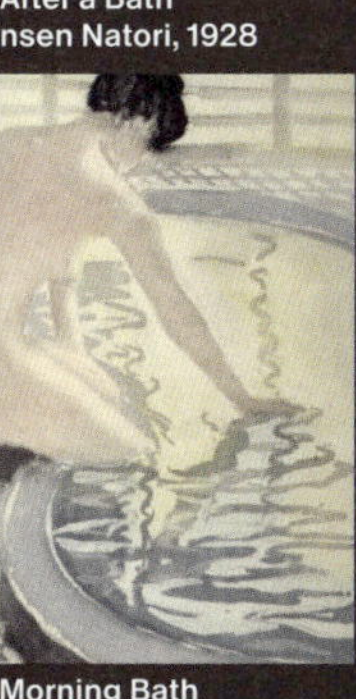

Morning Bath
ah Brayer, 1989

22 Onsen e Yukou!
Nakanishi Yasuhiro, 1997

23 Marvel vs. Capcom
Capcom, 1998

24 Spirited Away
Hayao Miyazaki, 2001

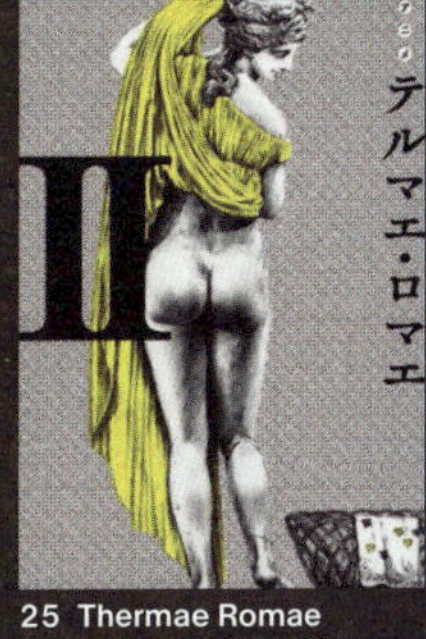

25 Thermae Romae
Mari Yamazaki, 2008

Onsen
温泉

The Hot Spring Law of 1948 defines onsen as natural water emerging from the ground above a certain temperature or exceeding a delineated amount of specific minerals. Composed of two characters literally meaning 'hot' and 'spring,' onsen are often found in more remote locations and traveled to as recreational excursions. The baths at onsen facilities are supplied directly from natural sources, either by gravity or through pumps, and chilled by the air on their journey to achieve an optimal temperature, otherwise heated, cooled, or diluted to arrive at a desired balance by adding water or through a boiler. Further differentiation between natural (tennen onsen 天然温泉) and man-made (jinko onsen 人工温泉) is clearly noted in the detailed display of water makeup and analysis usually framed just outside the entrance, and carefully supervised by regulatory agencies. The most coveted of the natural onsen, and highly prized by enthusiasts, are the free-flowing gensen kakenagashi (源泉かけ流し), which do not recirculate but rather constantly resupply unaltered water straight from the source.

With origins going back to the introduction of Buddhism to the country, onsen have become so synonymous with the culture of Japan that they could be considered a national pastime. But it is the wild onsen, in the middle of nature, that are tirelessly sought after, with some requiring multiple-day treks to arrive at. There is also a special classification of onsen establishments called 'Hitou' (秘湯), or 'secret hot springs,' a rare label reserved for only two hundred or so inns throughout the country that put an emphasis on protecting the natural environment, preserving traditional architecture, and maintaining a connection to the local culture. These destinations are known less for their digital obscurity than for their physical seclusion; while you might be able to easily find them on a map, actually getting there is almost always an adventure.

There are currently 27,932 hot spring sources in Japan – the highest anywhere in the world – while some remain untapped, others supply water to about 13,000 inns. Despite remaining popular destinations, these numbers have been in decline as sources dry up and operators struggle to find members of the younger generation, with their sights set on big cities, to take over what are typically countryside business locations.

Sento

銭湯

The Public Bathing Establishments Law of 1948 defines sento as facilities providing public bathing using 'hot water, seawater, hot spring, or other sources.' Made up of the characters for 'coin' and 'hot water,' sento are typically found in neighborhood locations and used for daily hygiene. They mostly use tap water that is heated by electricity, gas, or, in rare cases, the original method of wood-burning fires. Sento baths often contain artificially added minerals, medicinal herbs, and even fruits to enhance the experience. One main difference between sento and onsen is the source of their water, but there are also sento that pipe in onsen water transported long distances from far-off prefectures, blurring the boundary.

Sento have had such a long and storied history in Japanese society, used by emperors and commoners alike, standing in the face of local and foreign moral scrutiny, natural catastrophes and wars, that their current existence begs the thought 'if only the taps could talk.'

Unlike onsen, which have the liberty of setting their costs within ryokan (旅館 or 'inn') settings and are usually free when found in nature, sento have a tightly regulated fixed admission price controlled by ordinances in each prefecture. The cost of going to a bathhouse in Tokyo, for instance, has risen to ¥550, an amount that will date this book as it continues to slowly increase from its original price of ¥6 first established in 1948. For practical cleaning purposes, sento also favor using ceramic tiles instead of the wood and stone used in more traditional onsen.

There are currently only about 3,000 sento remaining throughout Japan, a far cry from their peak in 1968 when the number was closer to 22,000. Many different factors account for this sharp decrease, among them shifting societal tastes and generational preferences around privacy.

But there is reason to be hopeful. While sento have been on the decline for years, a relatively recent trend of modern renovations to these bathhouses, many of which are approaching the 100-year mark, has breathed new life into the industry. By including amenities that appeal to a younger demographic, such as sauna facilities and beer taps, updated sento designs have sparked renewed interest in the once-fading practice of communal cleansing.

黄金湯

KANTO 関東

Following the great Kanto earthquake in 1923, carpenters specializing in temple construction rebuilt public bathhouses that had been destroyed in the natural disaster. Sento in this region that proliferated in the aftermath of the quake feature iconic architectural flourishes closely resembling traditional elements of both Shinto shrines and Buddhist

temples, a style known as Miyazukuri (宮造り). This grand approach to bathhouse design has continued to this day throughout Kanto, notably in Kodakarayu (子宝湯), a historic sento immortalized at the Edo-Tokyo Open Air Museum, which one would be forgiven for thinking was a place of worship.

Curtain

The Noren (暖簾) curtain, seen hanging outside shop entrances, has fabric with a visible pole in Kanto.

Kerorin Bucket

The Kanto version of this famous water bowl has a diameter of 225 mm (8.9") and a height of 115 mm (4.5").

KANSAI 関西

In contrast to their northern counterpart, the architectural features of the bathhouses that populate the southern region of Japan's main island, known as Kansai, are less formal and even playful. The now-shuttered Gengahashi Onsen, which was built in 1937, used a mix of Japanese and Western elements in its facade. Most notably, in

Shibi

A roof decoration shaped like a Shachi (鯱) monster, with the head of a dragon and body of a carp.

入浴 (nyuu yoku)

Twin statues of liberty grace either side of the top entrance window, an homage to historic wordplay.

addition to the traditional roof decorations known as Shibi (鴟尾), there are two statues of liberty framing the center window, a tongue-in-cheek reference to the '入浴' characters, which are pronounced 'nyuu yoku,' meaning to 'enter a bath,' and sound just like the name of the famous city that houses lady liberty.

Curtain

The Noren cloth in Kansai hides the pole and tends to be longer than in Kanto, considered to be more elegant.

Kerorin Bucket

The Kansai version has a diameter of 210 mm (8.3") and a height of 100 mm (4"), so it is not too heavy when filled.

3
3

03

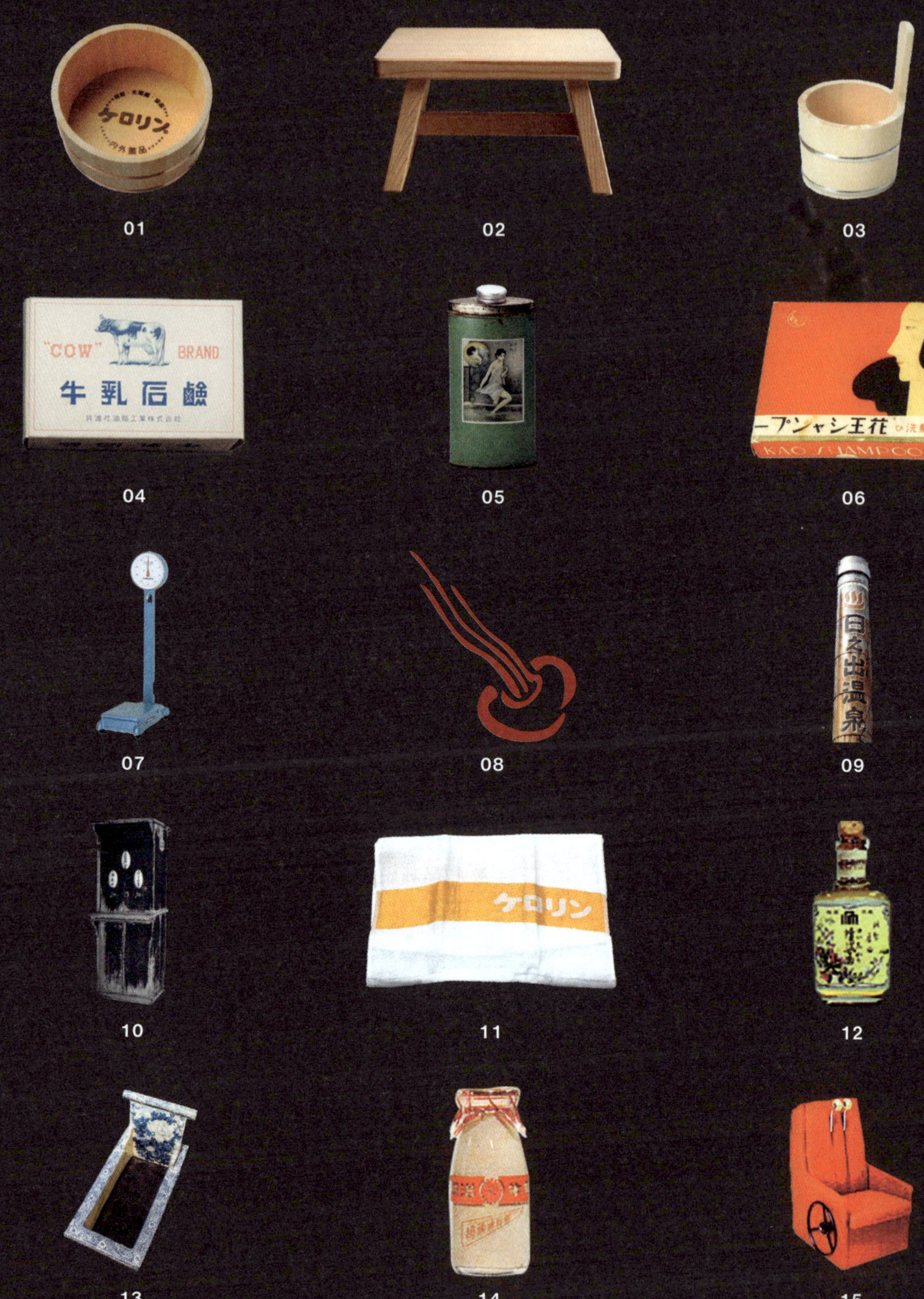

ONSEN ARTIFACTS OLD | NEW

The bucket, the stool, and the ladle – the holy trinity of bathing – assume their rightful place atop the pantheon of onsen artifacts. A number of other essential objects are also familiar to any bather in Japan, and while they have changed over the years, they retain their recognizable form, a silhouette of nostalgia with a patina of plastic: same item, new age. The onsen mark itself, found on the back of ancient

documents in 1661, has been redesigned several times to become the famous icon seen all over Japan today.

01 Bucket (桶), 02 Stool (湯椅子), 03 Ladle (手桶), 04 Soap (石鹸), 05 Salts (入浴剤), 06 Shampoo (シャンプー), 07 Scale (体重計), 08 Mark (記号), 09 Chimney (煙突), 10 Vending machine (自販機), 11 Towel (タオル), 12 Hair tonic (ヘアトニック), 13 Toilet (トイレ), 14 Milk (牛乳), 15 Massage chair (マッサージチェア).

WOOD 木

Wood is perhaps the most representative building material of traditional onsen. Specifically Hinoki (檜), also known as Japanese cypress, is a favored choice due to its durability, antimicrobial properties, and more importantly, its fragrance, an aroma well-known to many that is able to conjure tranquil scenes of rolling steam at a single scent.

STONE 石

As a cool gray counterpart to the warm brown tones of wood, stone is a favored material of traditional bathhouses for its resilience to weathering along with fire-resistant properties, making it an ideal container for onsen water. Izu Blue Stone (伊豆青石), is prized for its softness, but even more for the marine shade it reveals when wet.

2 PRESENT
現在

Towards a Nude Architecture　裸の建築

The Select

It is no coincidence that Japan has more hot springs than any country in the world. Located at the meeting point of four lithospheric plates in the 'Pacific Ring of Fire,' which contains roughly two-thirds of all the volcanoes (and suffers 90 percent of the earthquakes), almost one in ten of these fiery mountains calls the island country home. This seismic intensity results in a wide variety of hot springs, emerging from fissures deep beneath the ground to tell of the infernal mechanisms below, like geologic biopsies.

The select springs highlight a wide cross-section of the onsen that I have encountered in my years of journeying across Japan, from grand historic landmarks in town centers to remote shacks in forgotten landscapes, categorized by context: Mountain (山) | Valley (谷) | Sea (海) | River (川) | Forest (森) Field (田) | City (市) | Ruin (廃) | House (家) | Demon (鬼). Each location brings with it a unique relationship to the nature that birthed it into being, and is prized both for the quality of its waters and the beauty of its environment.

The onsen in this book span all four major islands and several prefectures, reflecting the particularities of their distinct land formations and architectural surroundings. Gunma has an amazing range of renowned springs, and Akita and Aomori are famous for their acidic waters and heavy snowfall. Hokkaido's crisp cold is the perfect pairing for intense heat, while Tochigi and Niigata have contemporary bathing facilities full of quirks and character. Ehime is home to what is widely regarded as the oldest onsen, and Kagoshima's distant islands offer some of the wildest

1 Sakinoyu Rotenburo at Shirahama Onsen.

bathing experiences there are. This coverage is intended to give both an introduction to the many different types of Japanese hot springs as well as to illustrate how their architecture is closely entwined in its surroundings.

In Japan, onsen are reminders of both the earth's tremendous power for destruction and for creation. More than anything, however, they are opportunities to deeply bask in the tectonic gifts of nature.

ONSEN TAXONOMY
Volcanoes and tectonic boundaries projected onto the selected onsen locations, illustrating the connection between chaotic movements in the earth's mantle and the precious mineral waters that emerge in the process.

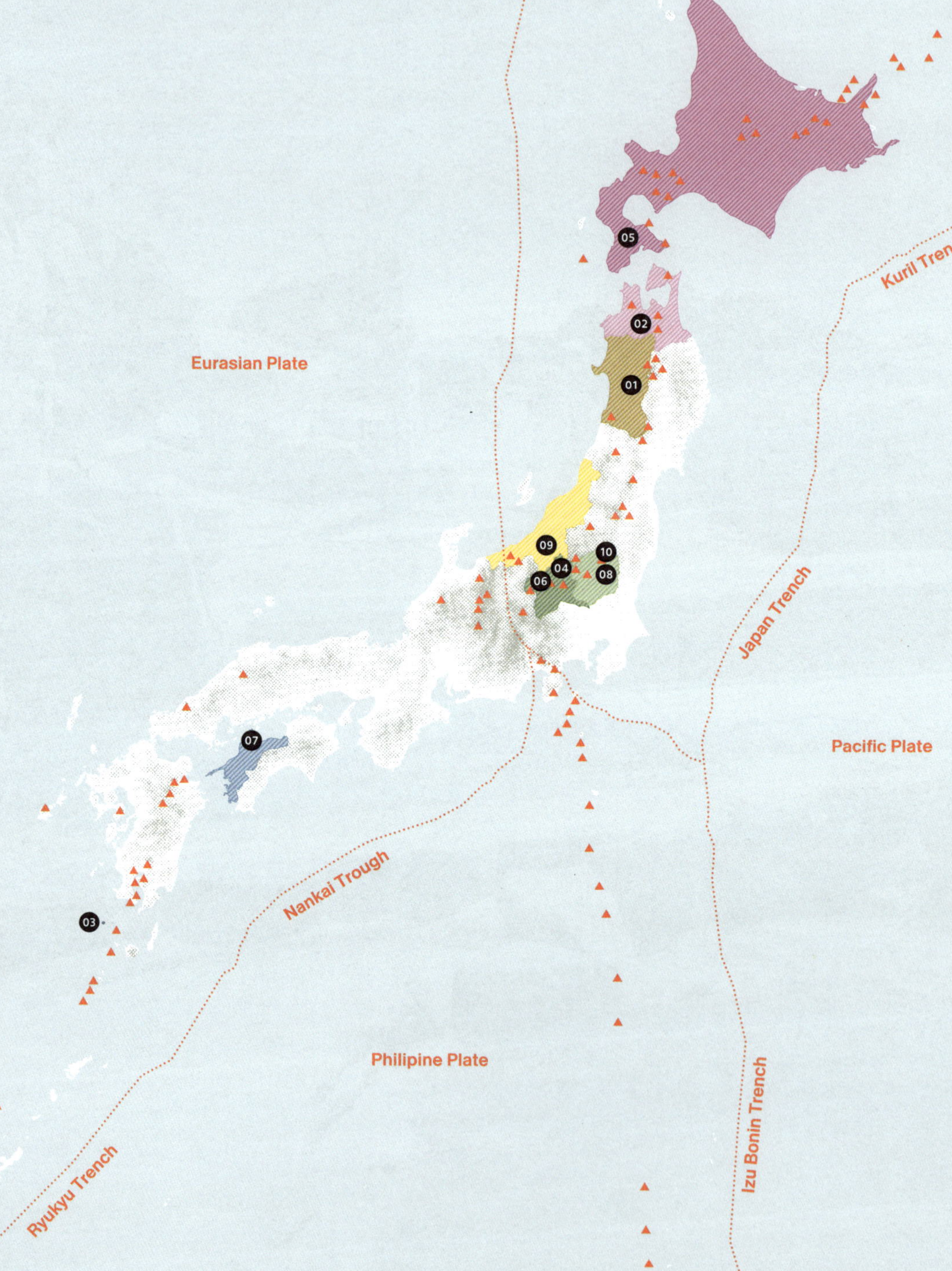

01 MOUNTAIN
Tsurunoyu

02 VALLEY
Aoni Onsen

03 SEA
Higashi Onsen

04 RIVER
Takaragawa Onsen

05 FOREST
Ginkonyu

06 FIELD
Kusatsu Onsen

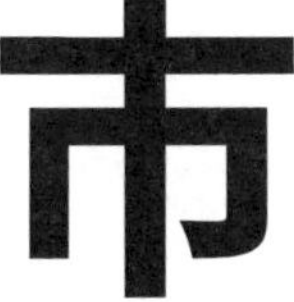

07 CITY
Dogo Onsen

08 RUIN
Oimatsu Onsen

09 HOUSE
House of Light

10 DEMON
Kita Onsen

MOUNTAIN

Tsurunoyu
鶴の湯

H_2O Sodium Chloride Bicarbonate | pH 6.6–7.1 | 39.4–46.8°C

Somehow both a staple centerfold in onsen literature and a stubborn secret of tight-lipped aficionados, Tsurunoyu Onsen in Nyuto Village so embodies the charm of the Japanese countryside that it would be difficult to find its description without the word 'rustic' liberally sprinkled throughout. This is only enhanced by its remoteness, nestled deep in the mountains of Akita Prefecture in northern Honshu, it is not an easy place to arrive at, even less so at its peak beauty in winter.

The hot spring's origin, as should be expected, is no stranger to lore. The name is derived from the myth of a local hunter who, when following the path of his prey, came upon an elegant crane (tsuru 鶴) healing its wound in the milky spring waters. From this inception, it gained further notoriety when the Lord of Akita began using the grounds as his private onsen in 1638, his troops stationed in the cottages that now house guests. The onsen ryokan opened to the public in 1688, and ranks among the oldest in the country.

Every corner of the inn exudes country comforts, from the steeply pitched thatched roofs of the wooden guesthouses that loom overhead, to the constantly smoldering hearth of black charcoal grilling freshly-skewered and salted Iwana trout. The highlight of it all, of course, is soaking in the prized waters of the outdoor bath, overflowing with the much-desired Nigoriyu (濁り湯) cloudy water. Tsurunoyu has five baths in total: three indoor baths – Kuroyu (黒湯) with black water, Shiroyu (白湯) with white water, and Nakanoyu (中の湯) – along with a women's only rotenburo and the famous large mixed rotenburo.

I visited during a winter storm in January. Mounds of snow had blanketed the buildings in a sheet of white, so picturesque that you would think the whole scene manicured, each snowflake intentionally placed. Months before, I had managed to secure a reservation over the phone in broken Japanese as I heard the pages of a thick, dusty tome turning audibly in the receiver. It was probably leather-bound. After arriving, I stepped out to take a midnight dip, sinking down to my neck in the sulfurous waters as a fluff of snow gathered on my head, naked and alone in the stillness of nature.

本陣鶴の湯

田沢湖乳頭温泉郷
秘湯鶴の湯

PRESENT 現在

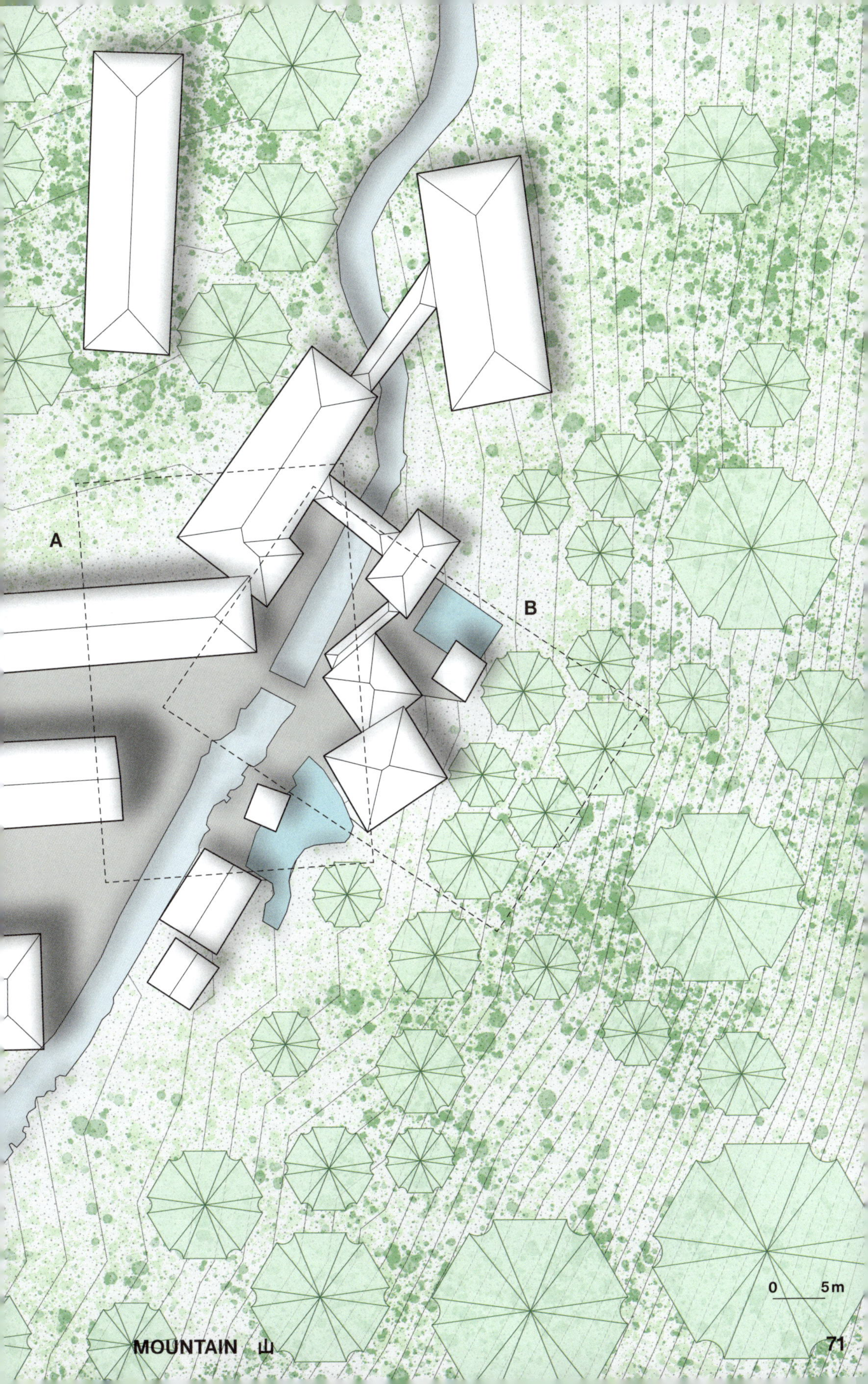
A
B
0
5m

PRESENT 現在

A

B

VALLEY

Aoni Onsen
青荷温泉

H_2O Simple | pH 7.4–7.6 | 41.7–48.2°C

If one finds themselves in Aoni Onsen, a remote ryokan hidden inside a snowy valley of Aomori, they won't be able to tell anyone about it. Also known as Lamp no Yado (Lamp Inn), this getaway has no internet or phone connection, uses no electricity, and is lit entirely by small kerosene lamps located throughout the site; a sensory deprivation tank ryokan. The toilets, however, still somehow maintain their magically heated seats, an apparent limit to the relentlessness of Japanese asceticism.

The complex, founded in 1929, features four baths of different character. Most impressive is Kenrokunoyu (健六の湯), an indoor bath made of aromatic hiba wood – a native conifer – with large windows facing what would ideally be a snowy landscape. A small stone rotenburo is situated silently facing the nearby mountain, practically buried in winter; a picturesque yukimiburo (雪見風呂) or snow-watching bath. There is a larger covered stone rotenburo with a small bathing barrel beside it, along with two more recently added baths inside. Each of the springs is lit by the same orange glow that unifies the entire site within the landscape. The steep-roofed wooden buildings of the lodgings are nearly invisible in the white of winter, blending in seamlessly with the surrounding trees.

I spent two reflective nights at Lamp no Yado, and they were some of the most introspective of my life, by force at first. But as the stay came to an end, among the stillness of the snow illuminated by warm globes of light, I found myself thinking, almost convincingly, 'I could get used to this.'

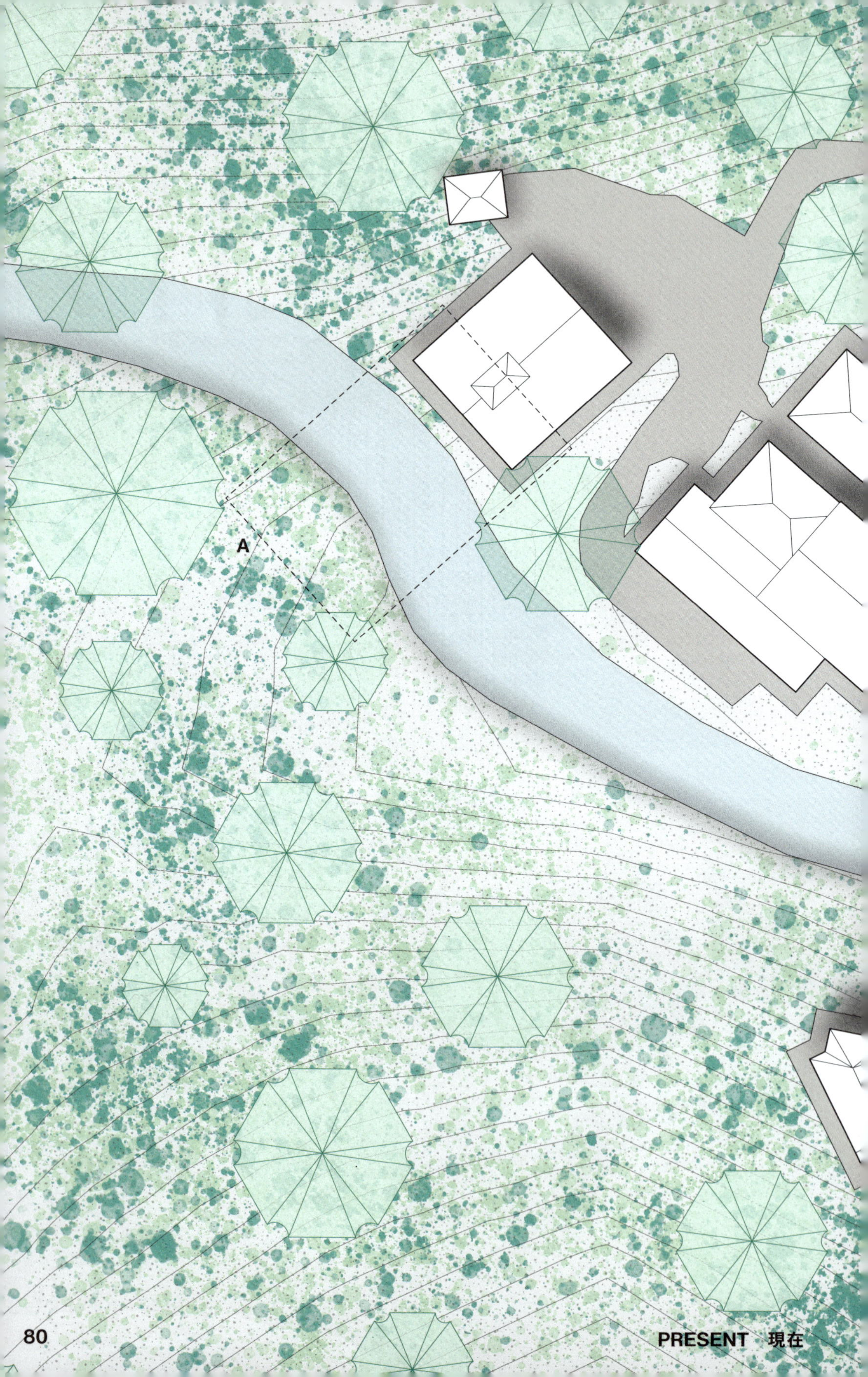
A

VALLEY 谷

子宝の湯

A

B

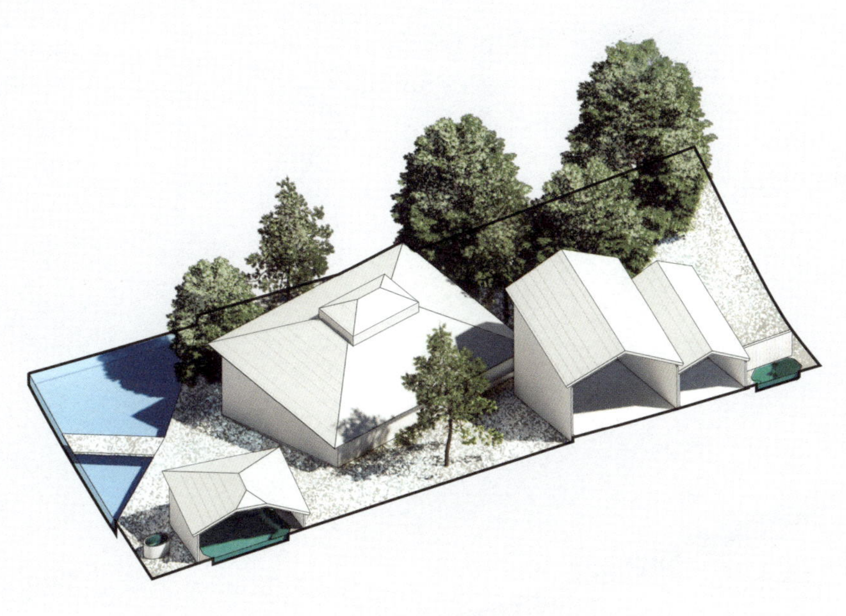

頭ぶつけな

SEA

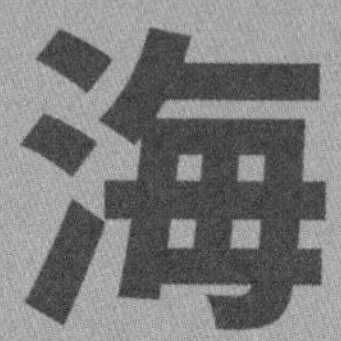

Higashi Onsen
東温泉

H_2O Sulfuric Acid | pH 1.7 | 47–55.8°C

Considered among the wildest hot springs in Japan, the trek to Higashi Onsen requires use of almost every form of transportation: a flight or train into the city, then a car drive to a small dock in Kagoshima, followed by four hours at sea on an irregularly scheduled boat, a bike ride through the tropical shrubbery of a nearly-deserted island, and finally, at long last, a short walk to arrive at this Mecca of Mizu (水).

All of the anticipation could make for a very anticlimactic dip, but Higashi Onsen is in a standing all its own. The three progressively hotter rotenburo pools are located on the south coast of Iojima (硫黄島), literally 'Sulfur Island,' a tiny spec floating between the Pacific and East China Seas. Half of the island is covered by Mount Io, a volcano coated in smoldering fluorescent yellow sulfur. When the tide reaches a certain height, the acidic emerald green mineral waters mix with the deep blue of the sea, creating a turquoise striation at the mingling; an intensely gradated embrace between two highly contrasting bodies of water.

The backdrop of this natural onsen is just as striking, with vegetated cliff faces seemingly plunging into the ocean. There are no facilities save a small changing room that appears like a ruin amongst the rocks, and no trace of human intervention other than the boundaries of the bath, which you could mistake for natural stone formations.

People often want to know what my favorite onsen is, and I usually tell them it's complicated before trailing off about the different categories as I sketch a tier list, their eyes glazing over with regret at having asked. If I am pressed to pick a single experience that was the most unforgettable, however, then Higashi Onsen would be it. And I say this without the slightest worry that the tiny island of 126 inhabitants will be overwhelmed by the revelation. In fact, after a few beers, I'll start talking about these springs to anyone who happens to be sitting next to me at the local Izakaya pub – usually a middle-aged Japanese guy who is quick to jot down the recommendation in between excited gulps of a whiskey highball. It's a long way away, and few will venture so far out for a soak. But those who do will find that, while the aphorism of journey over destination holds true, in this case, it is very much the destination.

A

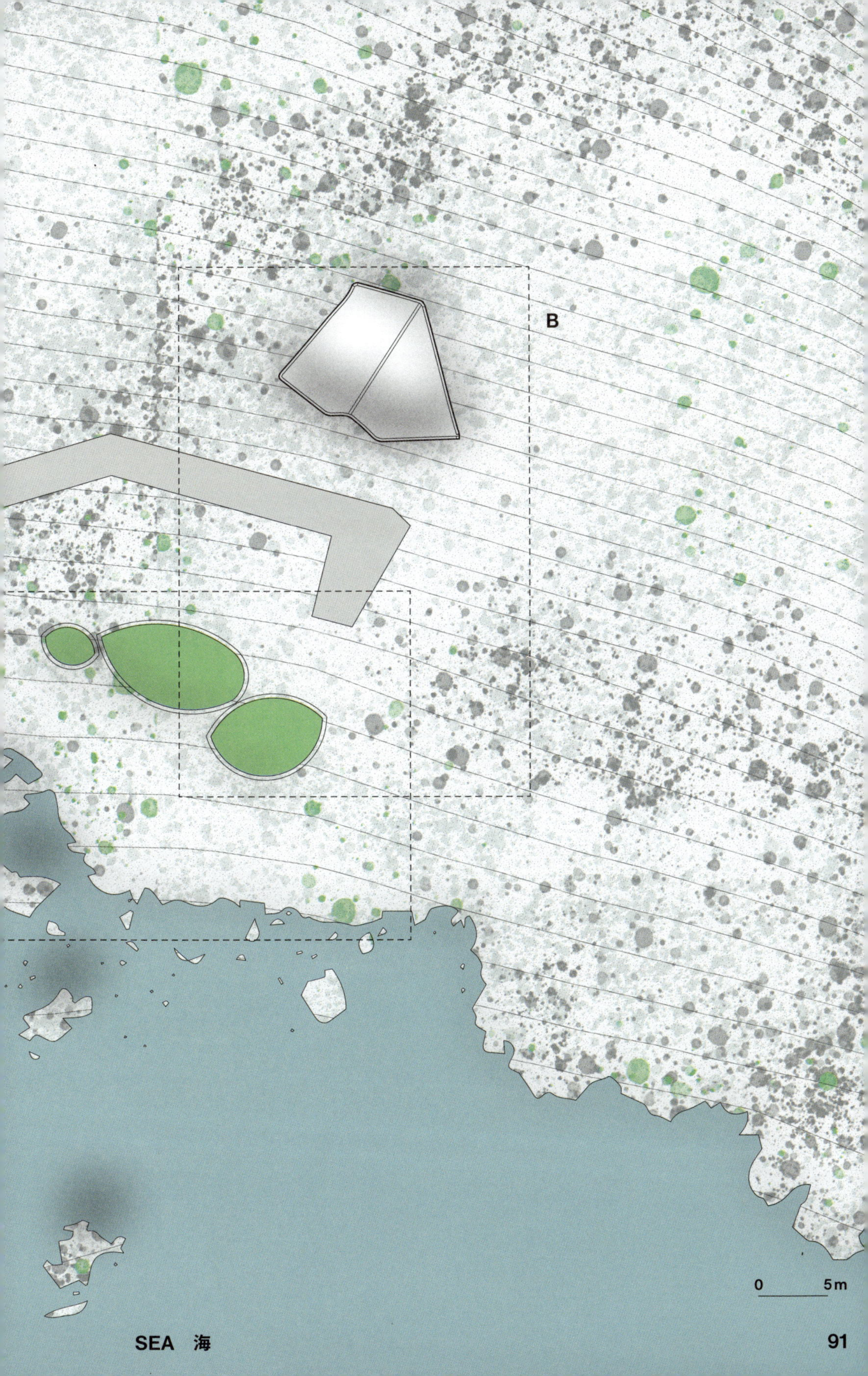
B
0
5m
SEA 海

PRESENT 現在

A

B

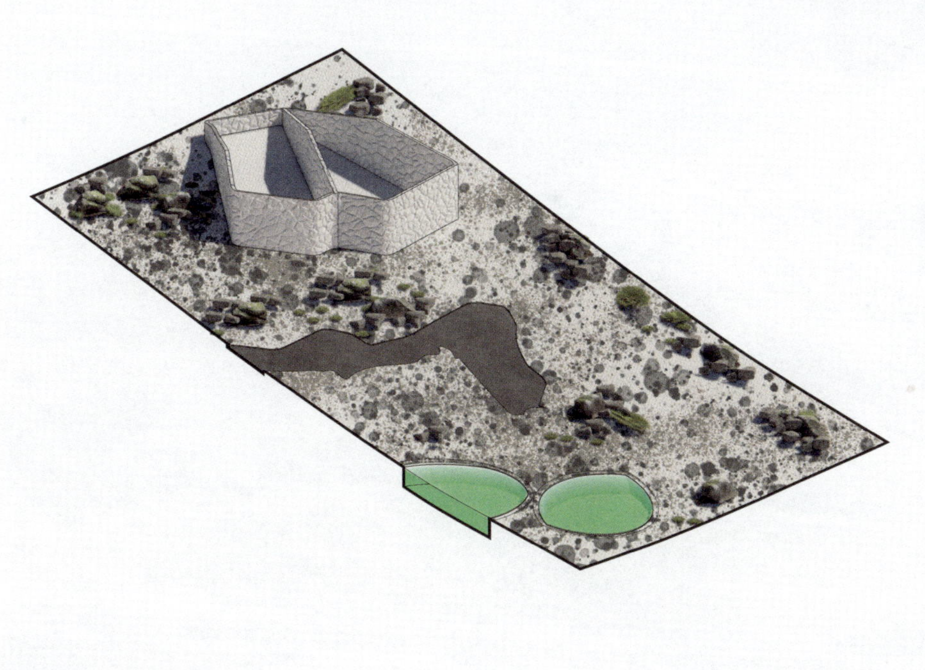

RIVER

Takaragawa Onsen
宝川温泉

H_2O Simple Sulfur | pH 7.7 | 40–43°C

It's difficult to answer which season captures the beauty of Takaragawa Onsen best. In the muted tones of winter, orange hues of autumn, or verdant greens of spring, these steamy outdoor baths tightly hugging a frigid river provoke audible sighs from those who've been there at the mere mention of the name.

One of the onsen with an animal origin story, which itself is a badge of honor, Takaragawa is said to have been discovered when Yamato Takeru – Japanese folk hero and semi-legendary prince of the imperial dynasty – happened upon a white hawk flying out in the distance. Following its path, he arrived at a hot spring which he declared Hakutakanoyu (白鷹の湯), or White Hawk Spring, the original name.

Takaragawa features some of the largest mixed-gender baths in the entire country. So big, in fact, that they are described in 'jo' (畳), a unit of measurement based on the traditional straw floor mats called tatami, which measure around 0.9m × 1.8m (3' × 6') in size and are typically used to describe room areas in buildings. Makanoyu (摩訶の湯) is 120 jo large and the most famous, frequently featured on television, in the backdrop of serial dramas, and in countless magazines and posters. A little further down is Hannyanoyu (般若の湯), measuring 50 jo and shallower, shaded by the canopy of a giant slanting tree. The largest of all is Kodakaranoyu (子宝の湯) which, at a massive area of 200 jo, is a luxuriously large field of water. Finally, Mayanoyu (麻耶の湯) is a women's bath of about 100 jo located towards the end of the site. All four rotenburo lie directly on either side of the rushing waters of Takara River. There are also separated gender baths inside the facility, which despite its own traditional charming wooden structure and adequately inclined roofs, plays a humble second fiddle to the scenery outside.

With my head resting on the cool stone bath rim watching the sun dip behind the trees, I closed my eyes to take in the subtle sounds of the riverbed. White or red, day or night, seen or heard, the magic of this onsen inevitably permeates all senses.

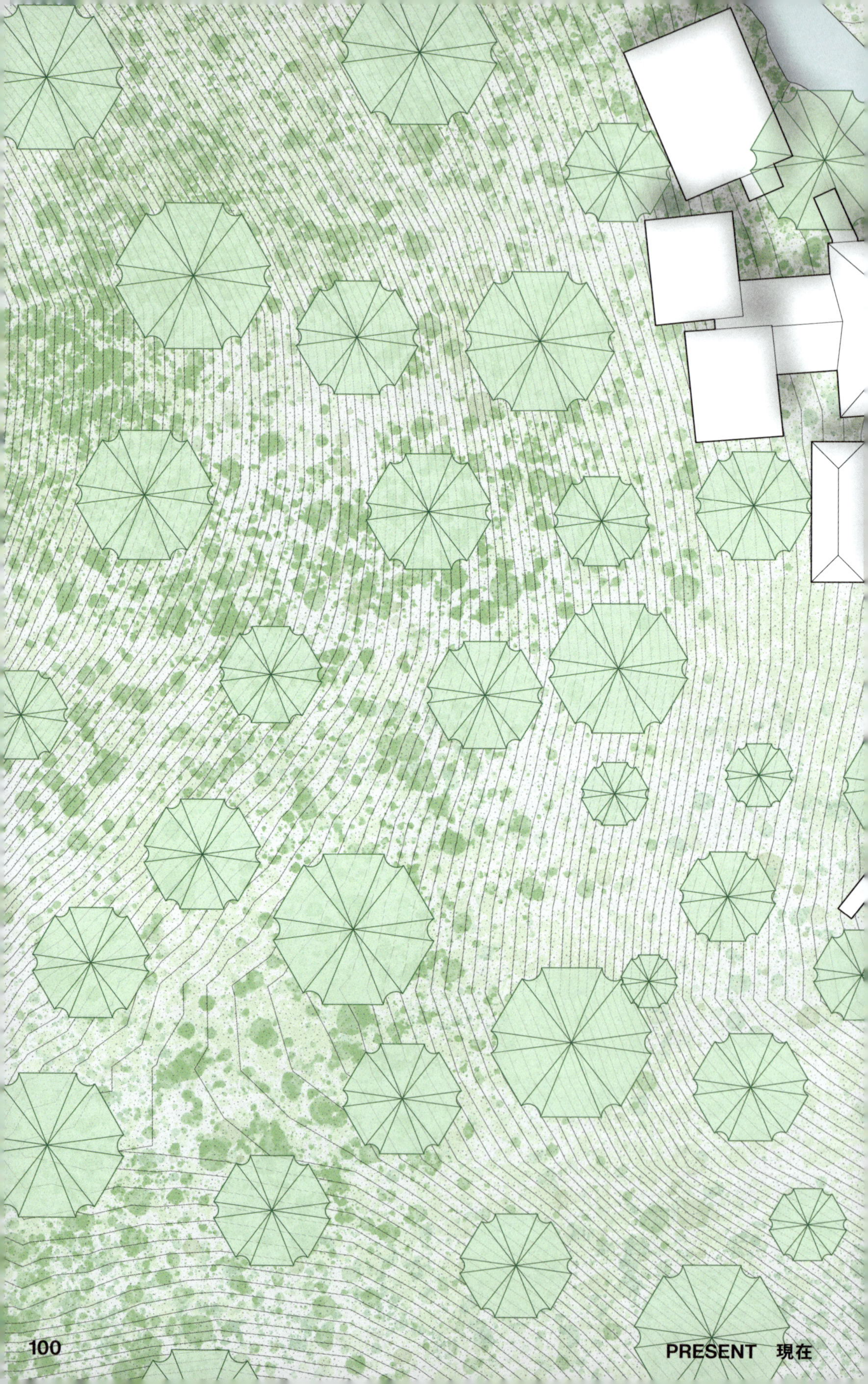

PRESENT 現在

A
B
0 10 m
RIVER 川

A

B

不動明王

FOREST

森

Ginkonyu
銀婚湯

H_2O Sodium Chloride, Bicarbonate | pH 7.1–7.3 | 41.6–44°C

There is a term in Japan called Shinrin-yoku (森林浴) which translates into 'forest bathing.' Coined by the Japanese Ministry of Agriculture, Forestry and Fishery in the 1980s, it refers to surrounding oneself in the grandeur of nature. In Ginkonyu, this concept is elevated to its most literal meaning.

Located in Hakodate, Hokkaido, and fed by a water source tapped relatively recently, the inn features a giant 16,000 m^2 (170,000 ft^2) plot of forested land with five private rotenburo pavilions completely integrated into the surrounding nature, each with its own quirkiness, like a Parc de la Villette for onsen enthusiasts. In these great outdoors there are two stone baths, including Momijinoyu (もみじの湯), which is rectangular, and Dongurinoyu (どんぐりの湯), which is round. Of the three wooden baths, Suginoyu (杉の湯) is a hut surrounded by trees, Katsuranoyu (かつらの湯) is a whimsical onsen treehouse of sorts, and the most famous, Tochininoyu (トチニの湯), is a hollowed-out tree trunk filled with water, facing the river. There are also several other baths, both indoor and outdoor in the main building, but the true experience is out in the wild.

Upon arrival, the guest receives a printed layout of the premises and a small wooden slab that acts as a key. The 'gates' of each bath are simply posts with a slot for that small slab – laughably innocuous in any other country as a form of privacy, but in Japan, this mostly symbolic boundary holds the utmost respect.

Still jet-lagged from a recent flight, I got up in the early hours of the morning, fastened the sash of my yukata (浴衣) robe, and headed towards the mixed-color canopies of early autumn. Leaving the map behind, I crossed the impressively long suspension bridge, ambled slowly through the well-worn trunks of the shirakaba white birch trees, and discovered by surprise the log bath in a small clearing. I hurriedly 'locked' the gate and, amidst the soundtrack of rustling leaves and running stream, eased myself into one of the greatest single soaks.

PRESENT 現在

FORESТ 森

PRESENT 現在

A

B

FIELD

Kusatsu Onsen
草津温泉

H_2O Chloride Sulfate | pH 2.0 | 50–90°C

Arguably the most famous hot springs in all of Japan, and a mainstay at the top spot of spring quality rankings, Kusatsu Onsen boasts the highest output and hottest temperatures in the entire country, with 32,300 liters of up to 90°C spring water gushing out every minute. There is good reason why the onsen town has claimed this position for so long – its bountiful, mineral-rich waters are delivered unadulterated directly from the nearby source of Mount Shirane, an active volcano. The area's best-known hotspot (literally) and the de facto center of town, is the Yubatake (湯畑), a bright blue/green 'water field' of seven wooden aqueducts that naturally air-cool the highly acidic sulfurous stream for distribution to surrounding ryokan.

Kusatsu Onsen is also a landmark spring of the therapeutic bathing movement. In 1876, Erwin von Bälz, a visiting German anthropologist and university lecturer, published a paper on the medical marvels of the town's waters, claiming that they could cure any disease. Indeed a common saying, possibly parroted from ancient folk songs, is that these waters, with their distinct mineral makeup, can cure everything but lovesickness. And even then, they could probably offer some help.

Drawing a constant crowd, one of the highlights is the Yumomi (湯もみ), a water mixing ceremony passed down for hundreds of years starting in the Edo period. This 30-minute event features women in traditional garb using large wooden paddles to cool the onsen water from 65°C to 48°C, maintaining the purity while making it inhabitable.

There are several ryokan and hotels where you can take in the award-winning waters, but the real gem is Sainokawara Rotenburo (西の河原露天風呂), a large 500 m^2 (5,380 ft^2) outdoor bath a short distance from the main plaza. The turquoise waters, so vast that you could swim laps, left my body revitalized, my mind rejuvenated, and, albeit partially, my heart mended.

PRESENT 現在

PRESENT 現在

A
0
20 m

A

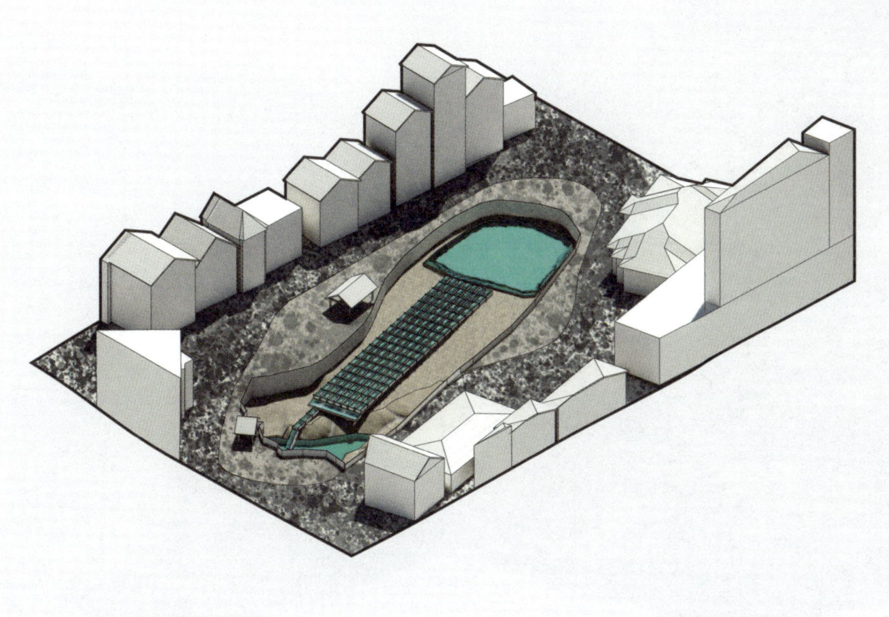

B

PRESENT 現在

CITY

Dogo Onsen
道後温泉

H_2O Alkaline Simple | pH 9.4 | 42°C

The title of oldest onsen in Japan is a contested debate. Sorting through stories of gods and mythical animals, testimonies of venerable nobility and acclaimed warlords, as well as recorded historical texts, however, has led to a narrowed consensus. There are two documents that refer to the 'Three Ancient Hot Springs of Japan,' or Nihon San Kotō (日本三古湯). The first is Nihon Shoki (日本書紀), translated as 'The Chronicles of Japan.' Finished in 720, it is the second oldest and most complete text of classical Japanese history, and mentions Dogo, Arima, and Shirahama onsen. The Engishiki Jinmyocho (延喜式神名帳), a list of shrines compiled in 927, references Dogo, Arima, and Iwaki Yumoto springs. Whether you take the origin legends at their word – a white heron healing its injuries in the springs (now immortalized as a statue sitting atop its highest point), or the god Sukunahikona no Mikoto curing his illness through bathing – the evidence remains that this is one of, if not the most ancient hot spring in the country, thought to have been discovered around 3,000 years ago.

The wooden three-story main structure was first built in 1894 and is the result of several expansions and renovations, evident in its copper roofs at various stages of oxidation that can be read as a building timeline. Dogo Onsen is perhaps the closest image that people have in their minds when they picture a Japanese bathhouse. This is not by chance; while many different onsen are rumored to be sources of inspiration for Hayao Miyazaki's 2001 masterpiece 'Spirited Away' (千と千尋の神隠し) – which introduced Japanese hot spring culture to an international audience – Dogo Onsen, with its dramatically sweeping tiled roofs, shoji lattice hallways, and overflowing tubs, is widely considered the most prominent.

The regal building houses just four baths, all worthy of its decorated history. Kaminoyu (神の湯), literally 'bath of the gods,' has a male and female version, and is not named in vain, with elegant stone tubs sunken below beautiful ceramic tile artwork. Similarly, Tamanoyu (霊の湯) has a bath for each gender, featuring a more subtle but no less refined design. The top two floors have generous tatami rooms for extended lounging post-soak.

I was lucky enough to be admitted late at night for an after-hours photography session where, among the many interesting nooks, I entered the otherwise off-limits women's baths. As the only soul strolling around a palatial bathhouse near midnight, I slowed my stride and swayed my arms exaggeratedly, taking on the affect of the princes and emperors that had once walked those same creaking floorboards. Arriving at the opulent waters, I raised my camera, the click of my shutter quickly snapping me back to reality.

道後温泉

PRESENT　現在

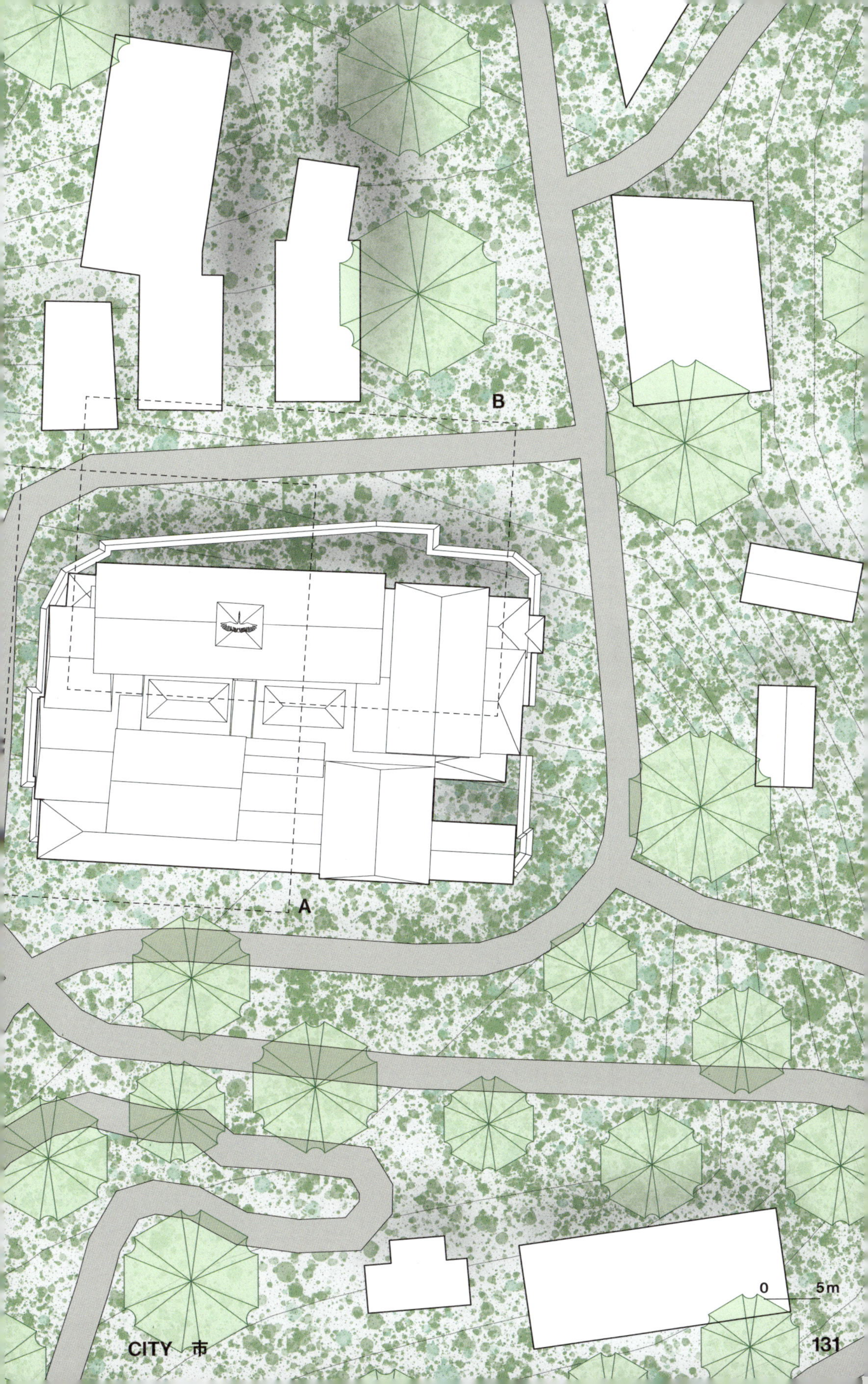
B
A
0
5m

A

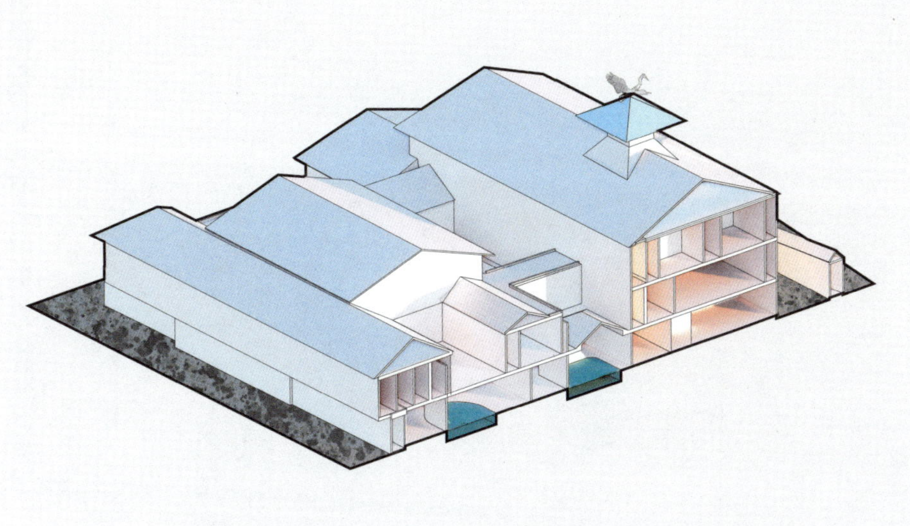

B

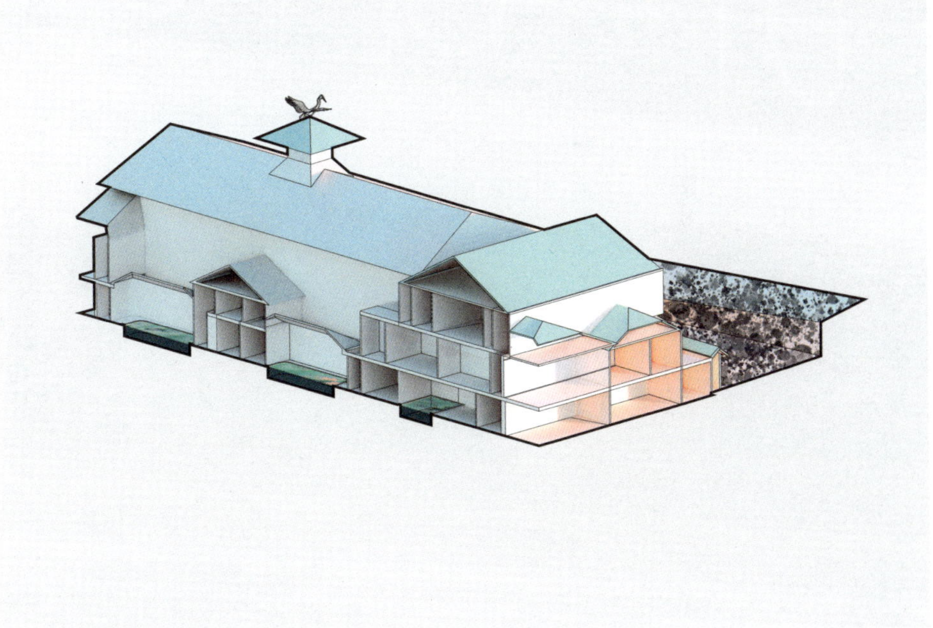

尊福

RUIN

Oimatsu Onsen
老松温泉

H_2O Simple Sulfur | pH 6.1 | 41.5°C

Oimatsu Onsen is the only hot spring in this book that cannot be visited. It no longer exists. The place itself was such a hidden treasure and the bathing experience so peculiar, that those who have the pleasure of recalling it might question if it was all a dream. Or nightmare.

This dilapidated wooden structure in the middle of nowhere had almost submitted to the surrounding vegetation before permanently shuttering in 2019, after over seventy years of business, though it seemed a few centuries older. If the exterior invited skepticism about the building's stability, the interior only heightened the trepidation, with cramped hallways and peeling wallpaper that any horror film location scout would be lucky to secure. The condition of the bathhouse was so perilous – it not only looked but felt like collapse was imminent – that niche corners of the Japanese internet had affectionately dubbed it 'dungeon onsen.'

By the time courage had been gathered to descend the expectedly creaky stairs to the baths below – one for men and one for women – the Hitchcockian anticipation was so thick that, well, it could have been cut with a knife. But then, at the very first dip of a toe, it all went away, the incredible contrast of ruin and steam somehow existing in perfect harmony. These lofty meditations, however, could only be held while the sun was still out. All poetic allusions quickly gave way to fear in the oncoming darkness.

After a long, winding trip, I arrived at what appeared to be an abandoned house. Just as my heart began to sink at ignored door knocks, however, there was some sudden movement inside. A tall man with a weathered face came out and, before I could say a word, waved me away. Initially rejected, I convinced myself that this was a good sign; he was trying to protect me from what would surely be my last bath. No, I decided, this was a test, the first of many. I explained I had traveled from far away specifically for the soak, and assured him that I knew the proper bathing etiquette. Thankfully, I was let in, and survived to tell the tale. Or at least I think that's what happened; memories become murky dwelling on this phantom spring.

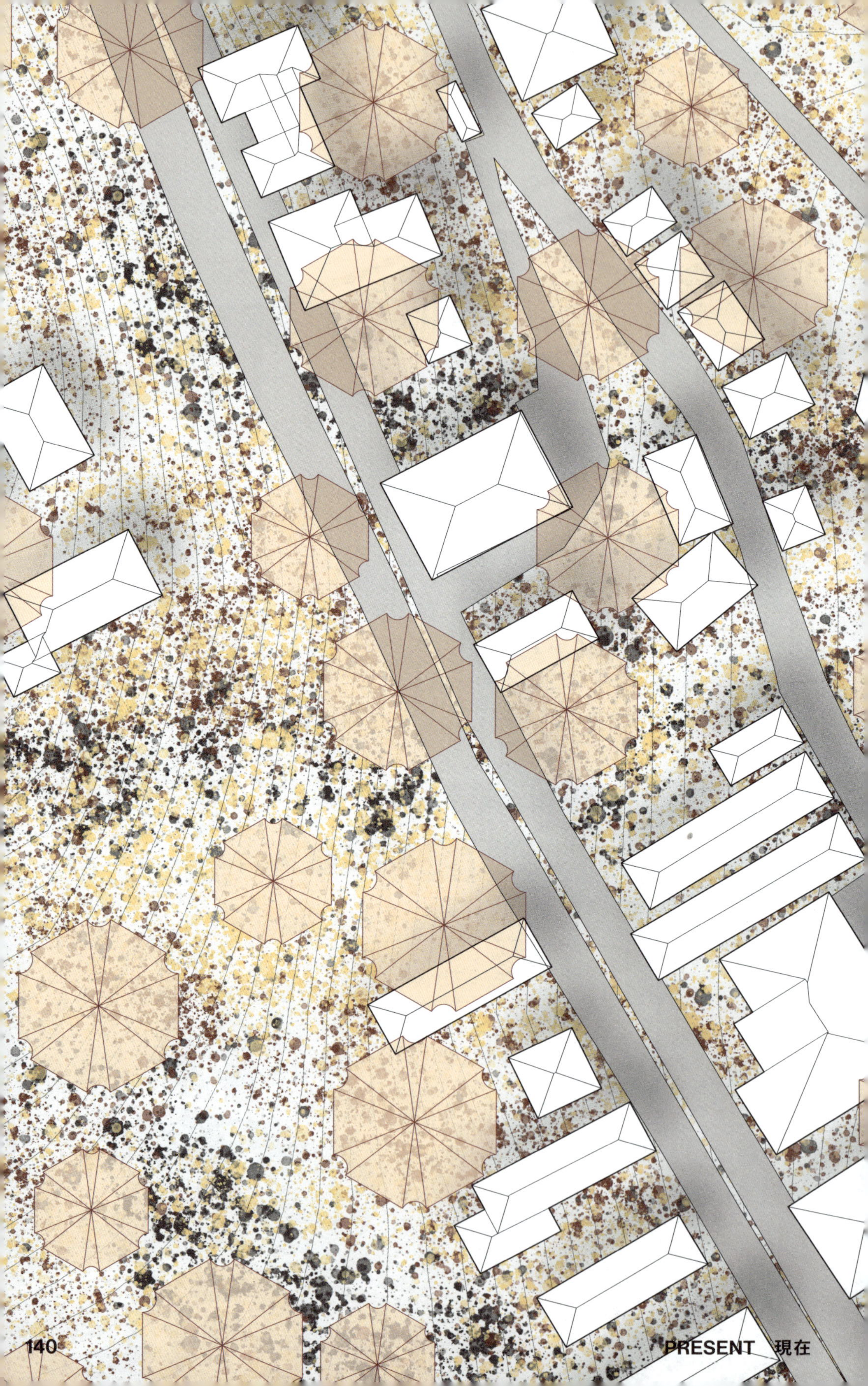

PRESENT 現在

A
B
0
10 m

PRESENT 現在

A

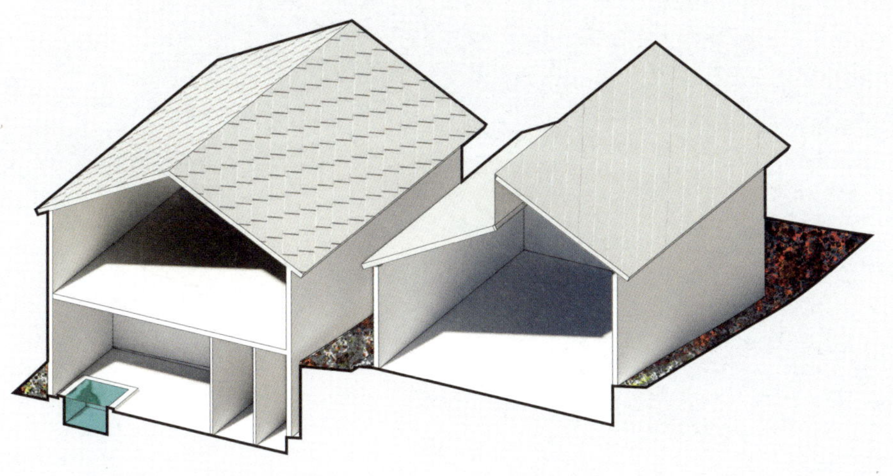

B

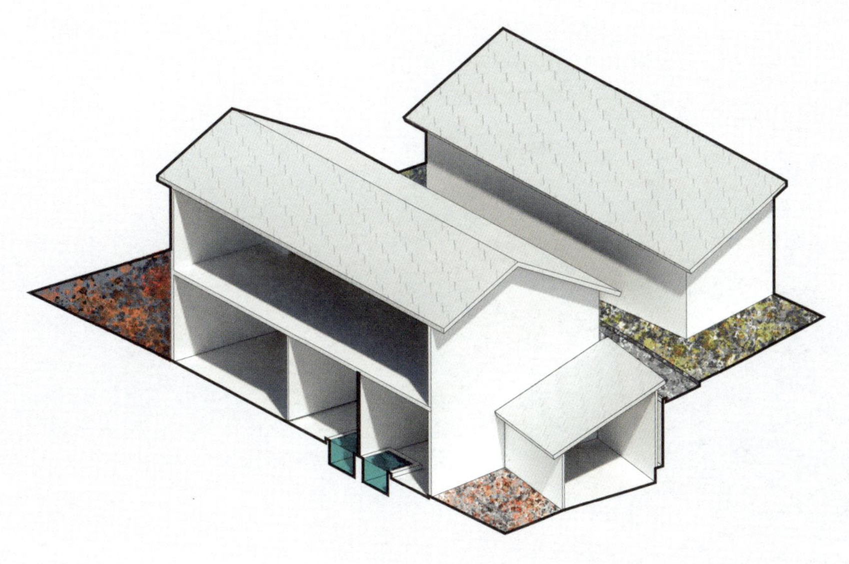

HOUSE

House of Light
光の館

H_2O Tap | pH 5.8–8.6 | 40.5°C

There are some who might consider the onsen of Japan to be works of art, but only a select few baths can wholeheartedly claim that title. Located on a terraced plot of land in the hills of Niigata, House of Light is an art installation that you can live in, a residence designed by the acclaimed 'master of light' James Turrell.

Built for the first Echigo-Tsumari Art Triennale in 2000, the work has a duality that can only be experienced on-site. By day, the house takes on the mild-mannered appearance of a traditional kominka (古民家), or a Japanese countryside stand-alone residence. In the shifting aura of sunrise and sunset, however, its true colors are revealed, transforming into an exhibition of illumination designed to complement the natural phenomena happening far beyond its walls. Removed from any light pollution and positioned to perfectly capture the moment, changing hues in the operable oculus roof frame the transition from day to night and night to day.

If this astral interplay on the second floor is the main show, then the bath downstairs is the afterparty. Red, blue, and green beams of light line the tub, casting an eerie glow on the entire scene. Although not technically an onsen as it uses heated tap water, in complete darkness – the recommended method of bathing here – all water looks alike. As my eyes adjusted to the room, like many of Turrell's works which gradually reveal themselves to slowly widening pupils, the small step at the lip of the bath changed from resting bench into spectator seat. The real celestial event was about to begin.

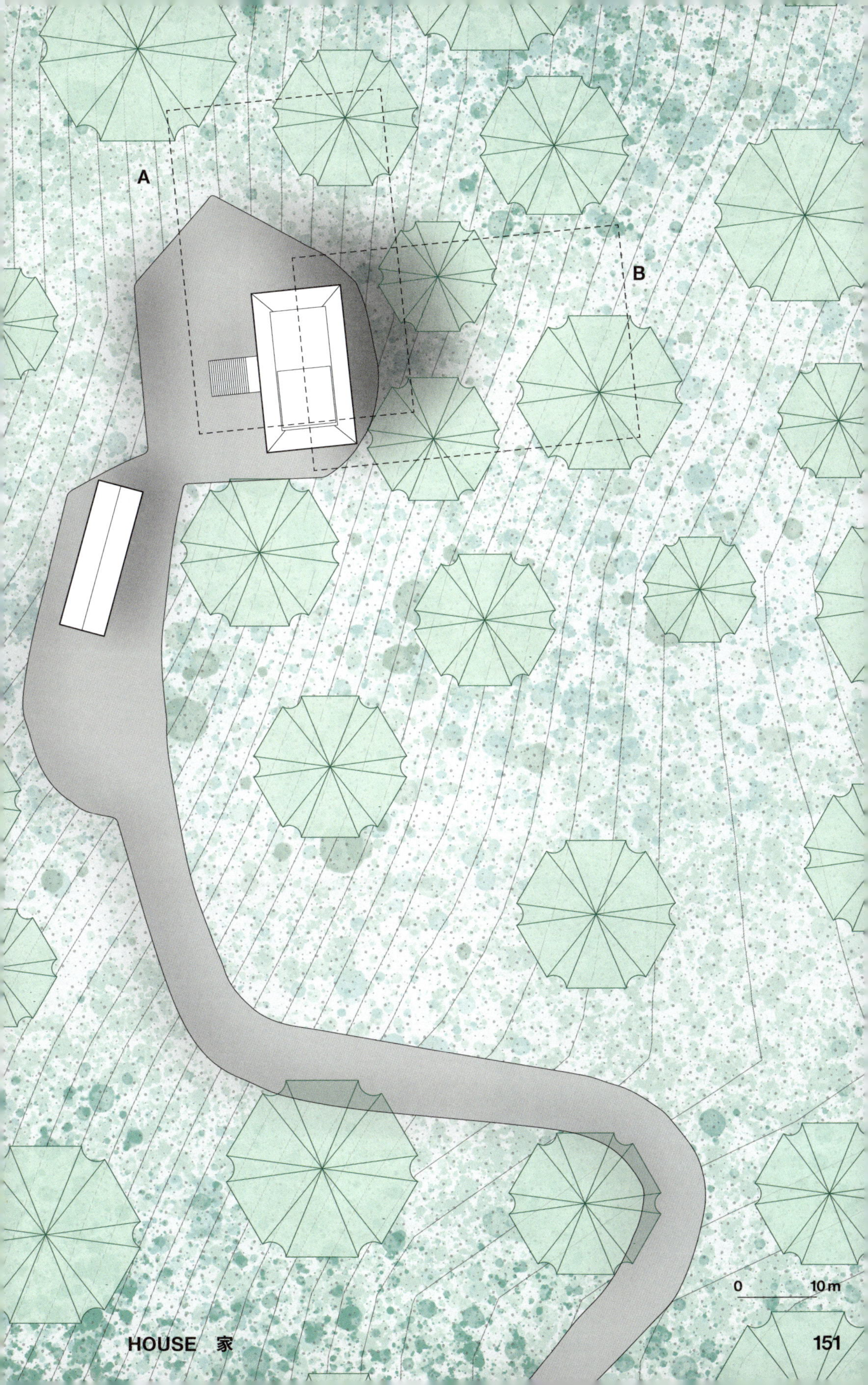
A
B
0
10 m

A

B

DEMON

鬼

Kita Onsen
北温泉

H_2O Simple, Sodium Chloride, Iron | pH 6.2–6.7 | 33–44°C

There is no shortage of remarkable onsen in Tochigi Prefecture, but Kita has a bath unlike any other. Driving along the winding Nasu countryside roads, a series of unassuming wooden buildings appear in the distance, composed of three main structures each built in different eras: an architectural collage of Edo, Meiji, and early Showa. As the quiet countryside atmosphere focuses into view during the short walk from the parking lot, it does not give so much as a suggestion of the demonic dip that awaits inside.

Local legends tell the story of the spring being discovered around 1,200 years ago by a 'Tengu' (天狗). Literally 'heavenly dog' in name, but demon in reputation from their ill-omened Chinese origin, these creatures have evolved into local folklore as supernatural vermillion-faced goblins with a signature long nose. In homage to this history, the oldest and most famous bath at this ryokan is named Tengunoyu (天狗の湯), where two colossal tengu masks keep constant watch.

Kita Onsen has a total of seven baths gravity-fed from Takinoyu (滝の湯), the hot spring source behind the site. In addition to the monstrous bath, there is Menoyu (芽の湯), the women's indoor bath, Ainoyu (相の湯), separate indoor baths for men and women, Kawaranoyu (河原の湯), separate open-air baths for men and women, and the huge rotenburo Oyogiyu (泳ぎ湯), so big that it is called a 'swimming bath.'

It was the unremarkable scenery of an aging interior contrasted with the hypnotic yellow-eyed stare of the tengu that drew me in. The floors, walls, and windows had not so much been neglected as they had been well-worn from use, with a texture of dings and cracks as forensic evidence of a thousand satisfied soaks. The bright red and vibrant blacks of the tengu masks, contrastingly, looked as if they had just been cleaned and polished in preparation for my arrival, making the entire space feel strangely preserved. Something was certainly in the details, whether devil or god I could not say.

PRESENT 現在

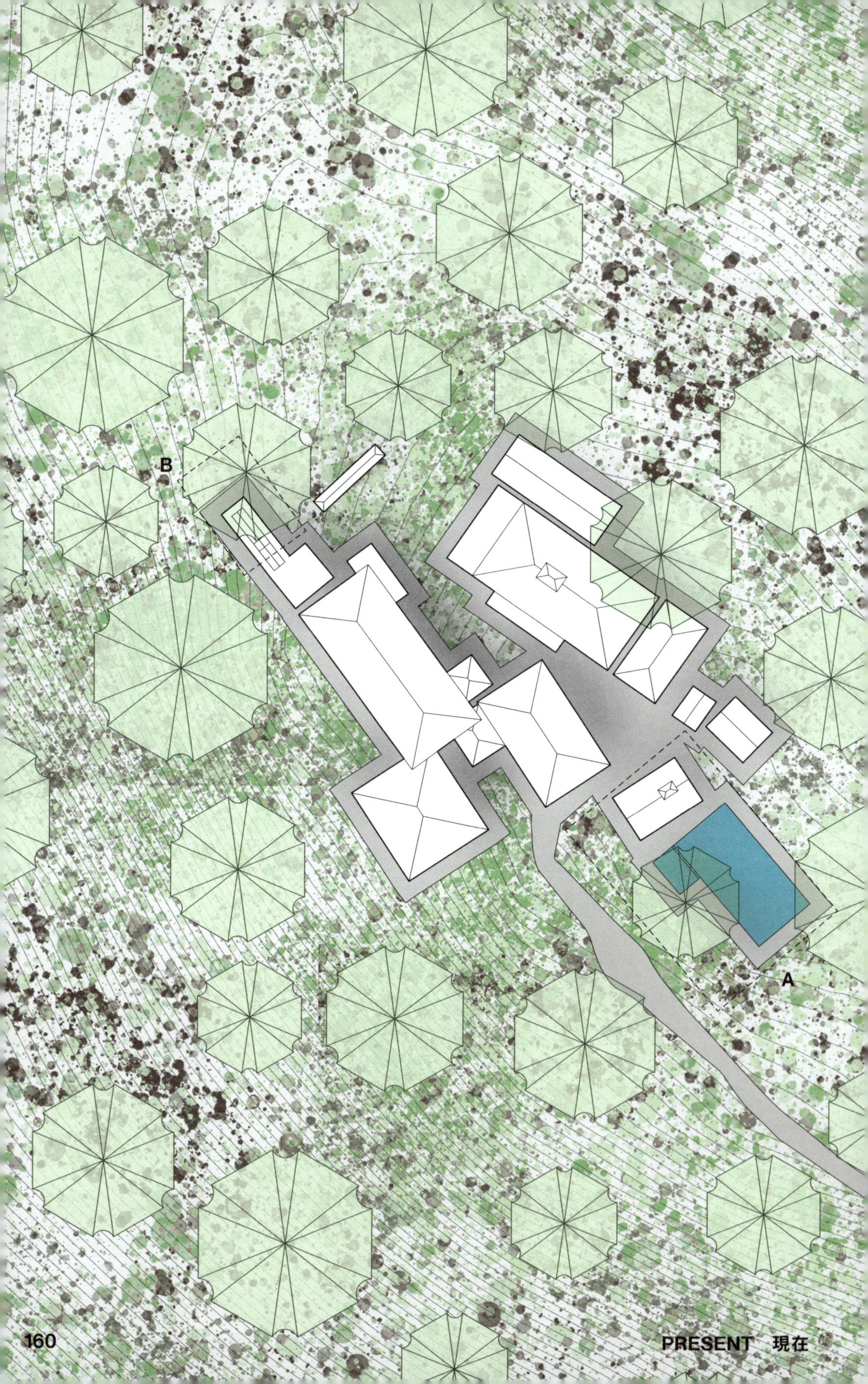

PRESENT 現在

0
10 m

PRESENT 現在

A

B

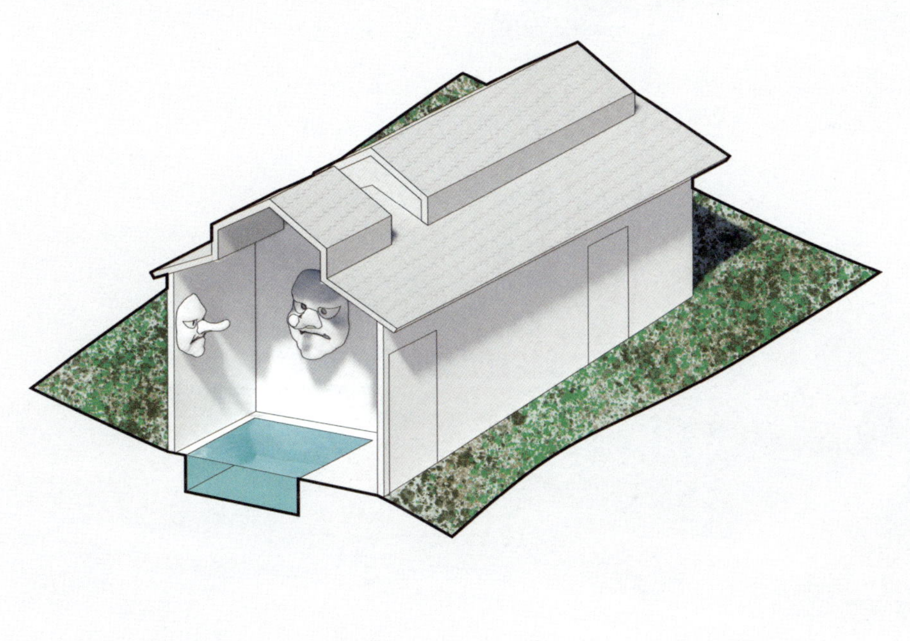

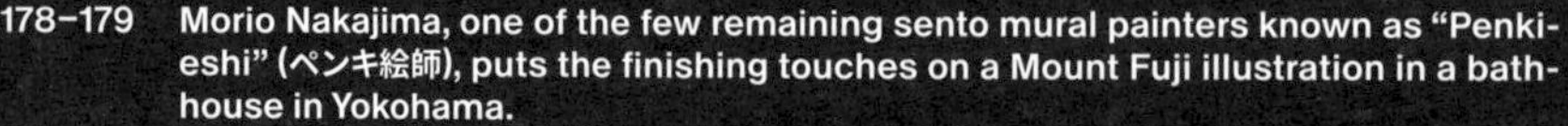

178–179 Morio Nakajima, one of the few remaining sento mural painters known as “Penki-eshi” (ペンキ絵師), puts the finishing touches on a Mount Fuji illustration in a bathhouse in Yokohama.

182–183 Meiji’s beloved Mount Fuji strawberry chocolate, inspired by the famous Hokusai print.

3 FUTURE
未来

ONE WAY
ONE WAY
FIRE LINE DO NOT CROSS

City of Steams

With a deeply tumultuous past and constantly fluctuating present, it might seem disingenuous to ruminate on the future of Japanese hot springs with any expectation of accuracy. Although onsen and sento numbers have suffered downward trajectories in the last near century, the coming chapters in their epic millennia-long story are not necessarily bleak. Perhaps the best way to make an objective prediction on what might unfold would be to, conversely, look at the topic from the outside. Or rather, the opposite end.

Digging straight down through the bountiful soil of Yugawara – the small hot spring town that I currently call home – all the way through the earth's core and back out, you wouldn't exactly arrive in New York, but you would be close. Although not the geographical antipode, it is the city where I lived when I first began formulating the idea for this book, which came after years of intermittent trips to onsen around Japan during nearly a decade of working in Asia. Back in the States in 2022, as I was developing an initial draft, the floor of my small West Village studio began to shake in a low, constant tremor. Concerned at this strange sensation, rhythmically distinct from the syncopated rumble of the subway, I rushed across the hallway and hurried down the stairs, a distant 'hiss' growing louder with each step. Once at ground, I pushed open the apartment door and arrived at one of the wildest scenes I have ever witnessed: an entire city block engulfed in a cloud of steam.

"This is going in the book."

1 2022 steam pipe explosion in New York's West Village.

The New York Steam Company began providing service in lower Manhattan in 1882, and today, ConEdison operates the largest commercial steam system in the world, although it would remain a secret if not for the sporadic bursting pipes that paint the streets white. While Manhattan's relentlessly gridded urban parcels might at first seem like the antithesis of a natural hot spring haven, these two seemingly unconnected physical and cultural utilities – heat generation and communal bathing – are, upon closer investigation, a natural match: the perfect catalysts for an urban social steam.

This closing chapter explores a selection of iconic Japanese bathing infrastructure and design – the heat source, the fuji mural, the communal and private bathing experience – and proposes an architectural reinterpretation (not quite) halfway across the world.

Nyuu yoku (入浴), Japanese, verb: to 'enter a bath.'
New York (ニューヨーク), English, noun: City of Dreams.

FIRE LINE DO NOT CROSS
FIRE LINE DO NOT CROSS
FIRE LINE DO NOT CROSS
FIRE LINE DO NOT CROSS

2

3

2–3 Steam chimneys are a common site throughout Manhattan.

4

BEPPU

You will smell Beppu before you see it. The infamous sulfurous 'rotten-egg' sting hits the nostrils right before a vista of wispy columns rising from what appears to be every other building comes into view, like man-made cloud factories. Once you've gotten used to it, which is surprisingly quick, the skyline should already be in full focus: a city shrouded in steam.

Located on the southern island of Kyushu in Oita Prefecture, Beppu, known as Japan's onsen capital, is celebrated for the sheer abundance of its springs, home to over 2,300 sources which account for almost ten percent of the total number in Japan. It is also renowned for the diversity in its spring quality, with seven of the ten major mineral spring groups represented. The city is home to a variety of bath typologies, from murky mud baths to sand baths and historic steam baths, as well as a secret spring tucked inside a hidden valley past a cemetery.

Japanese onsen towns like Beppu use intricate systems of deep-earth drills, pumps, and pipes to transport precious onsen water at ideal temperatures to hotels, ryokan, and private residences. Connecting to the source involves a base setup fee along with a monthly upkeep cost, a small price to pay for pure onsen water delivered directly to your tap.

Beppu even has an 88-onsen pilgrimage, a wink and nod to the famed Shikoku 88-temple pilgrimage. The reward for a completely filled 'Spaport' is a black towel with initials monogrammed in golden threads, the ultimate onsen trophy.

4 Billowing steam clouds form Beppu Onsen's iconic skyline.

EJIW
CON
EDISON
CO
MADE IN USA

5 

NEW YORK

Few New Yorkers realize that every waking moment they are walking, cycling, and driving atop the largest steam network in existence, a convoluted matrix of underground pipes that supplies hot air to over 1,700 commercial and residential customers, heating and cooling buildings, humidifying museums, and cleansing restaurant dishes.

Stretching from Battery Park to Manhattan's Upper East and West Sides, ConEd's giant steam machine comes with huge infrastructural and operating costs that can only be justified in densely packed metropoles. The technology de rigor at its inception, New York's steam complex has expanded to become the creaking, hissing subterranean behemoth that keeps the city that never sleeps up and running. The iconic orange and white stacks that can be spotted throughout the island, located at strategic points to lower the pressure on the system and literally let off steam, are usually the only visible signs of the hidden labyrinth of steel below. Once in a while, however, a pipe explodes – 2007 pictured above – sending a violent reminder of its size and ferocity.

New York also has a long history of public bathing, stemming from the lack of adequate facilities in the tenements of the nineteenth century. In 1851, the city's first public bathhouse opened on Mott Street, and while the last public bath closed in the 1970s, today both old and new commercial bathing venues continue to thrive. Albeit more luxurious than its aging bathhouse institutions, which proudly wear their charm on the walls, New York's current communal bathing resurgence is increasing momentum.

5 2007 steam pipe explosion in Manhattan.

FUJI MURAL

The famous Fuji mural that decorates the walls of countless sento around the country is said to have originated from a quaint Tokyo bathhouse named 'Kikaiyu.' In 1912, the owner of this sento commissioned a painter by the name of Kawagoe Koshiro to create a drawing inside the bathing area in order to attract more customers. Coming from Shizuoka Prefecture, where Mount Fuji is a constant backdrop, Kawagoe drew inspiration from the scenery of his home town and started a national trend with the stroke of his brush.

Following the success of Kawagoe's work, which made bathers feel immersed in nature, there was a proliferation of different subjects depicted by sento artists on this exciting new canvas within an emerging profession called penki-e (ペンキ絵). By mixing four basic colors of common house paint (white, yellow, red, and blue), these painters would illustrate vivid oceans, falling foliage, and even giant advertisements that subsidized their own cost. But it was the picturesque peak that remained the most popular image, with the layout of the sento themselves changing to place baths against the walls instead of at the center to strengthen the illusion of mountain-side soaking.

Drawing increased crowds of all ages at the height of their popularity, the prevalence of sento murals began waning towards the latter half of the 20th century, becoming a custom mostly centered around the Kanto region.

冨嶽三十六景
凱風快晴

のののののののののののののののののののののののののののののの
のののののの ののののののののののののの
のののののののののののののののののののののののののののののの
のののののののののののの ののののの
のののののののののののののののののののののののののののののの
のののののののののののののののののののののの
のののののののののののののののののののののののののののののの
のののののののののののののののののの
のののののののののののののののののののののののののののののの
ののののの のののののののの
のののののののののののののののののののののののののののののの
のののの ののののののののののののの
のののののののののののののののののののののののののののののの
のののののののののののののののののののの
のののののののののののののののののののののののののののののの
のののののののののののののののののののののののののののののの
ののののののののののののの ののの
のののののののののののののののののののののののののののののの
ののののののののののののののののののののの
ののののののの ののののののののののの
のののののののののののののののののののののののののののののの
'Red ののののののののののののの のの
Fuji,' or ののののののののののののののののののののののののの
its full name ののののののののののののののの
'Fine Wind, Clear ののののののののののののののののののののの
Morning,' is a woodblock ののの ののののの
print by Japanese artist Hokusai, ののののののののののののの
one in a series of 'Thirty-six Views of ののののののの
Mount Fuji.' Along with Hokusai's other print, のののののののの
'The Great Wave off Kanagawa,' it is perhaps the ののののの
best-recognized piece of Japanese art in the worldののの
and the most ubiquitous depiction of the famous mountain. The graphic has had a long-standing influence on the art community as an inspiration to impressionism and post-impressionism movements that arose in the following decades, and to the culture at large as an icon gracing the pages of the Japanese passport, postage stamps, and chocolate aisles. The print continues to enjoy widespread acclaim, prominently displayed throughout the country including, of course, interpretations in neighborhood sento murals.

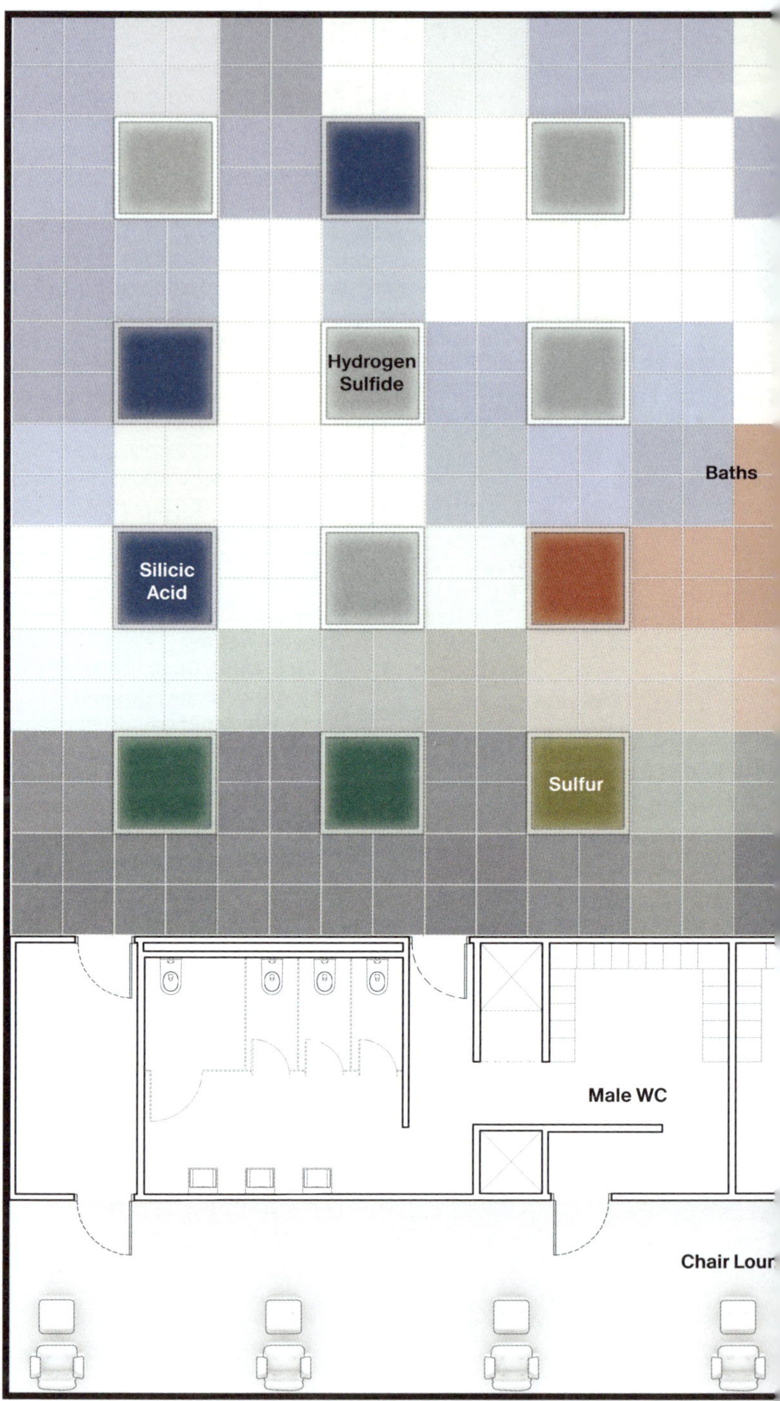

I ♥ 入浴 PLAN

'I Love Nyuu Yoku,' meaning 'I love to bathe,' is a proposal for a New York bathhouse heated by the underground Manhattan steam network.

Ground level entry with glass shoe storage turns the occupancy into a facade decoration. A rooftop balcony includes a bar overlooking the city, featuring the iconic New York water tower as an inhabitable private bath that proudly displays the symbol of a Japanese onsen to become the building's 'chimney.'

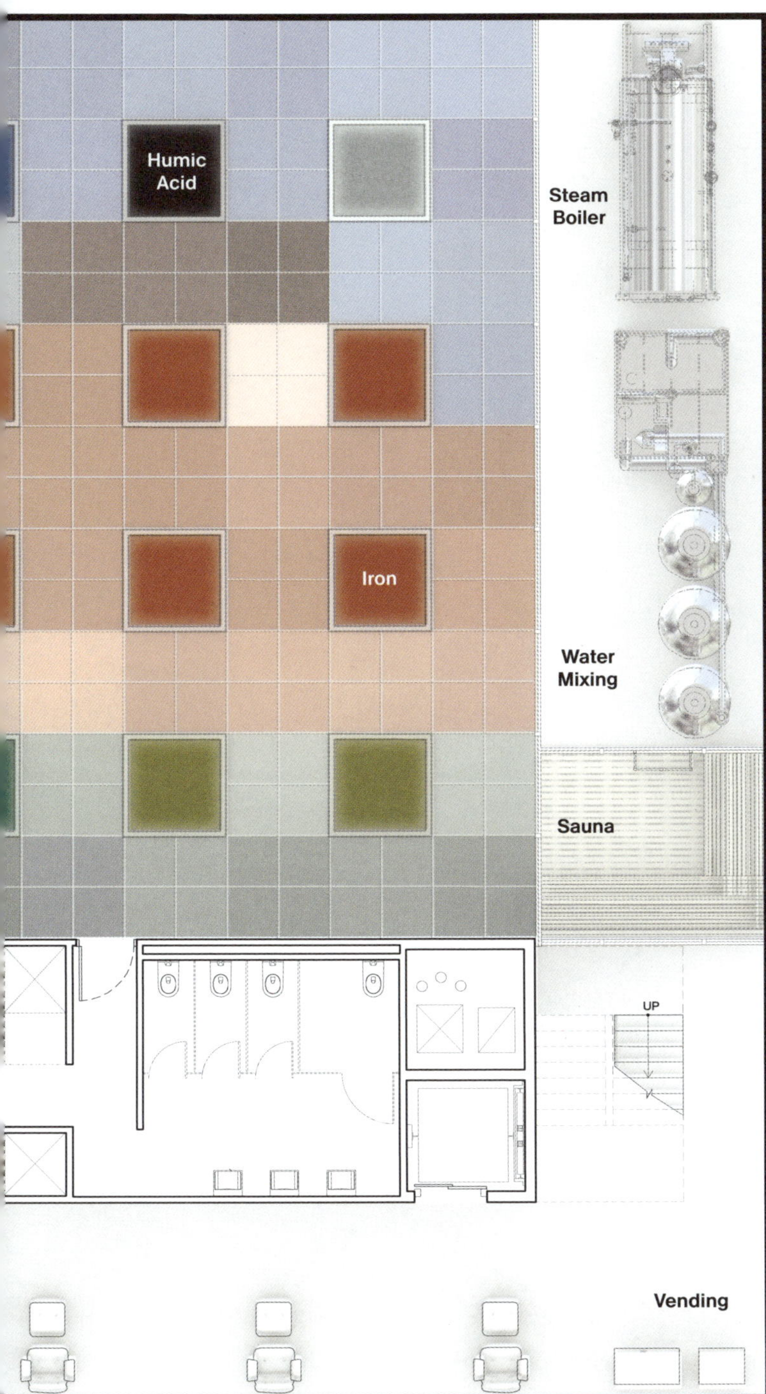

The bathhouse in the basement flips the Fuji mural horizontal, turning the quintessential sento graphic into a giant floor mosaic, with baths of different minerals as its pixels.

While just the sketch of an idea, this hybridizing of two cultures and elements, East and West, steam and water, could yield exciting social benefits in a city looking to sustain and invigorate its communal program to transform into the City of Steams.

I ♥ 入浴 SITE

The proposed site is located on a prominent strip in SoHo on Broadway, the oldest north-south main thoroughfare in the city. Formerly the Victoria's Secret New York flagship that closed down in 2020, the removal of the underwear (store) would symbolically usher in a new bathhouse for the city.

6

7

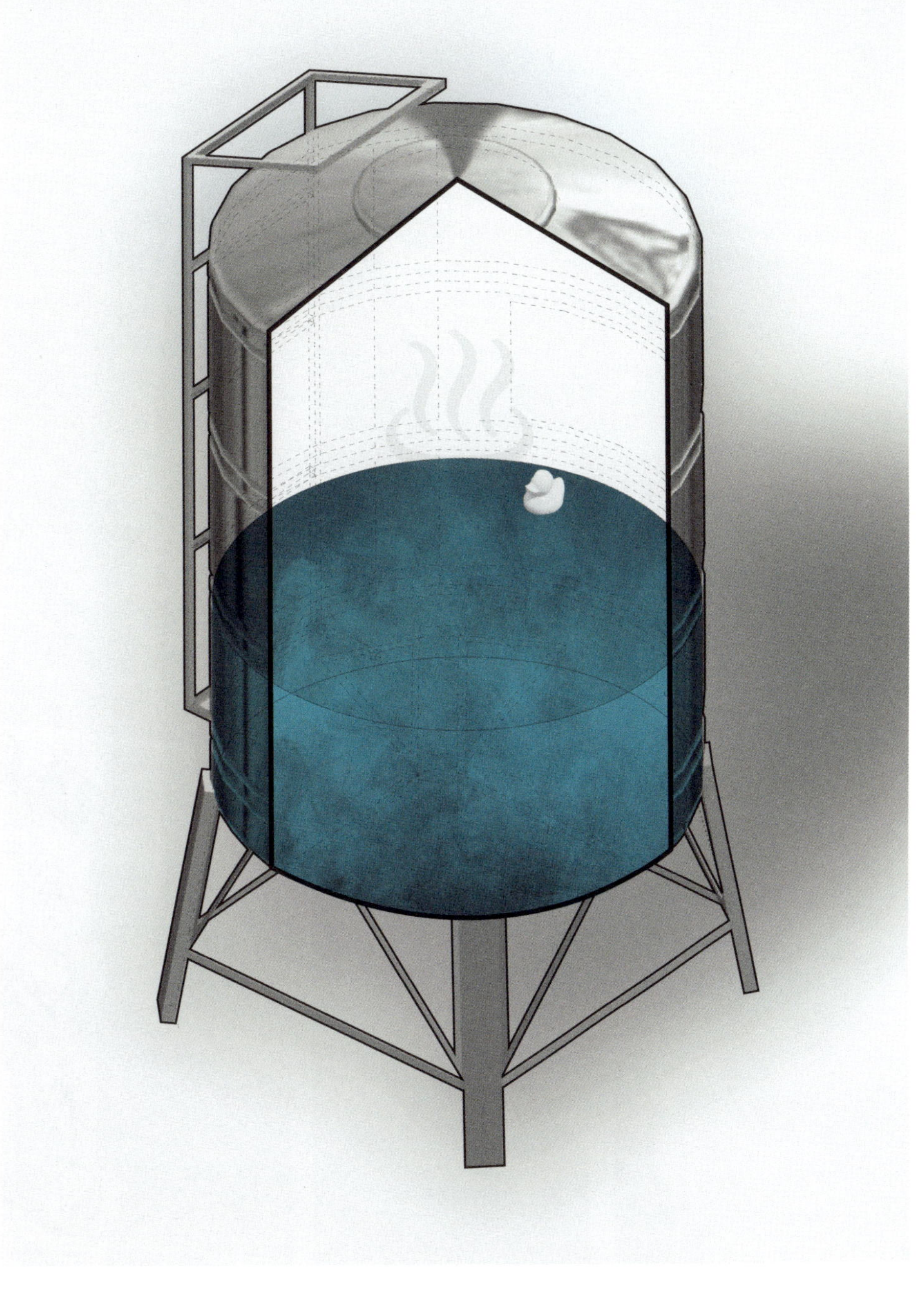

6 New York Water Tower.
7 Chimney Bath Isometric Section.

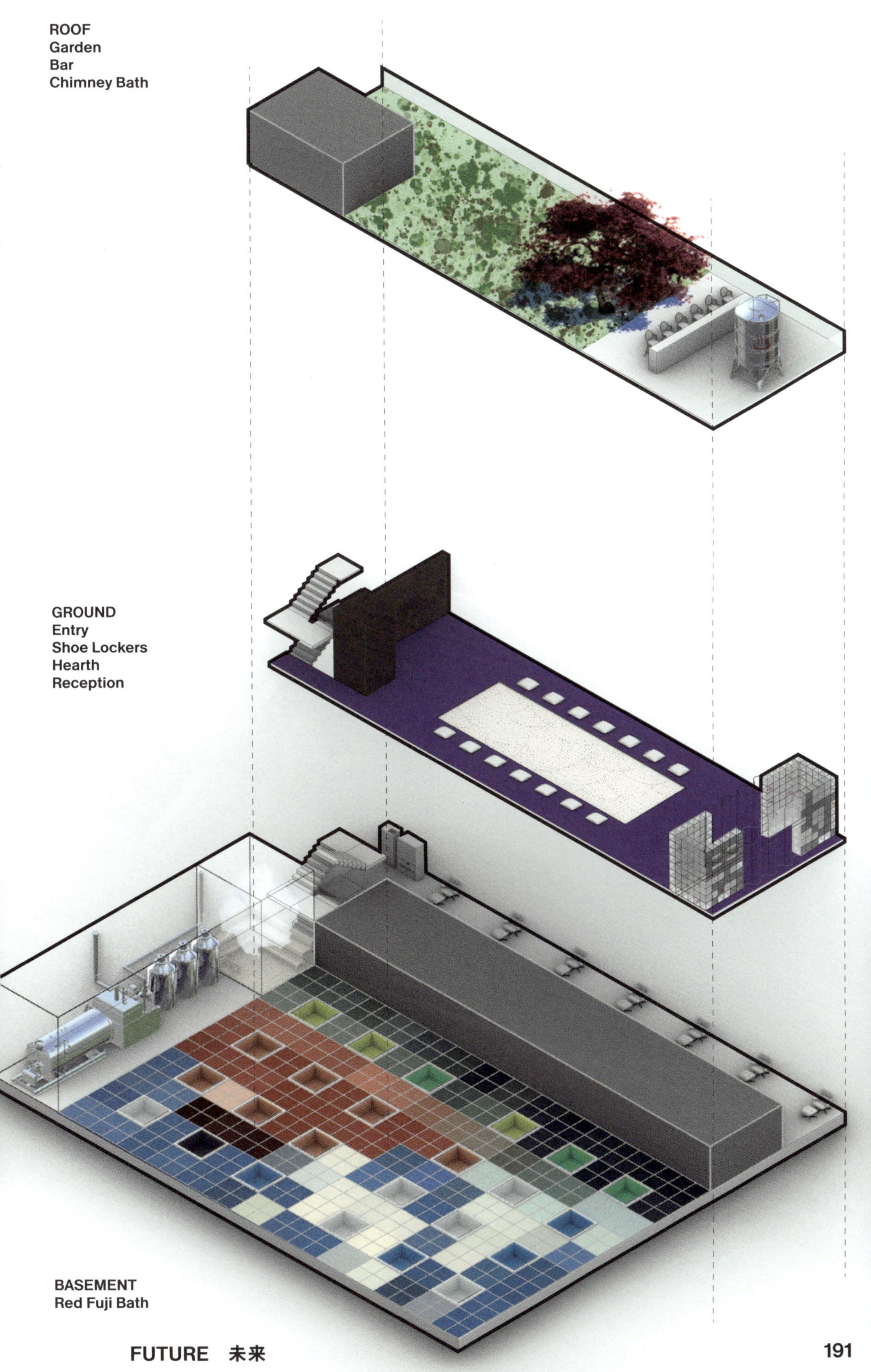
ROOF
Garden
Bar
Chimney Bath
GROUND
Entry
Shoe Lockers
Hearth
Reception
BASEMENT
Red Fuji Bath

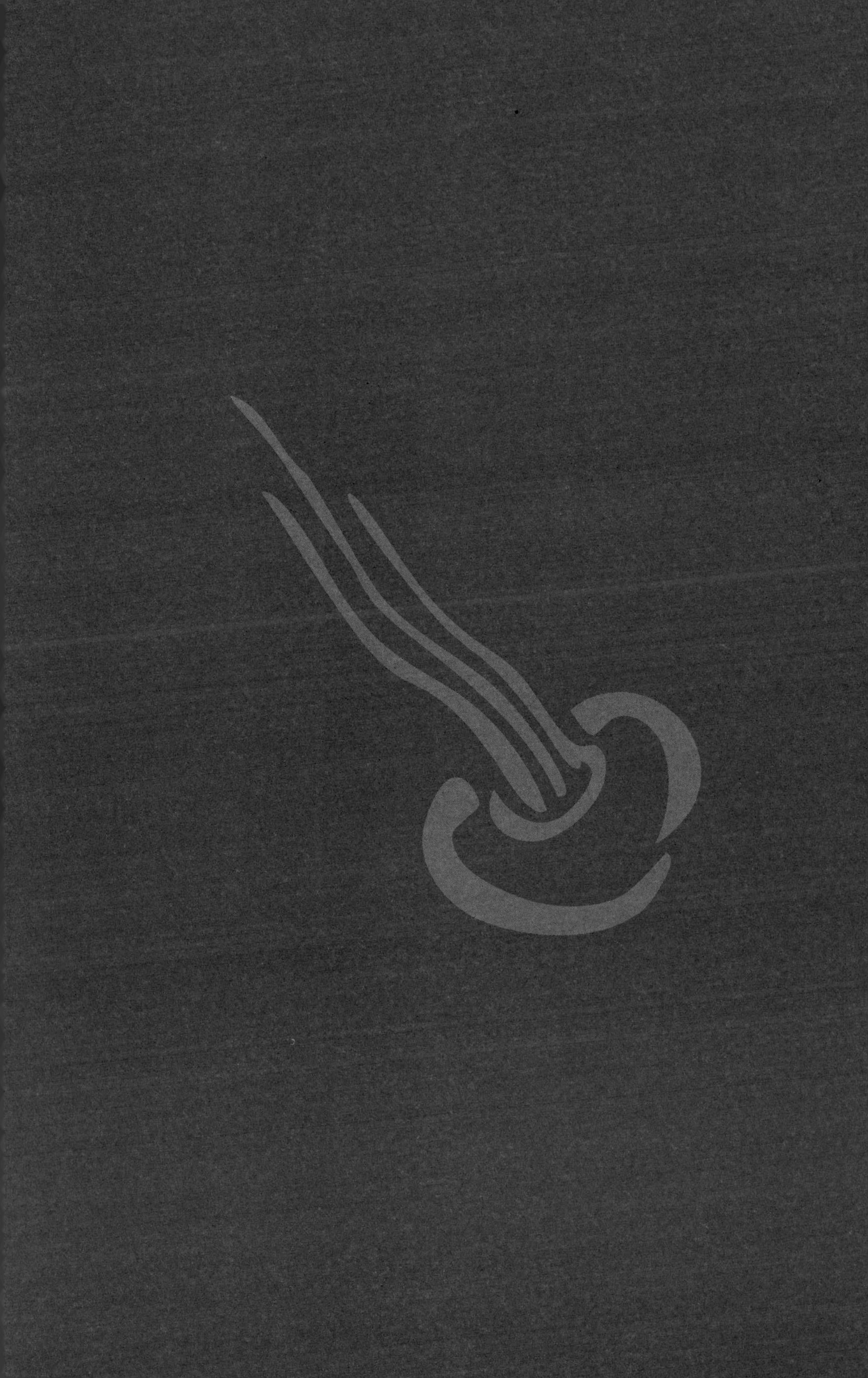

Index

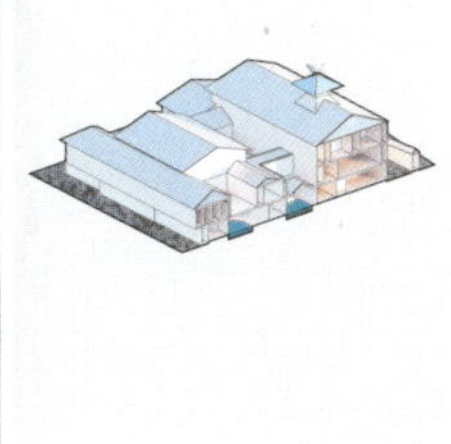

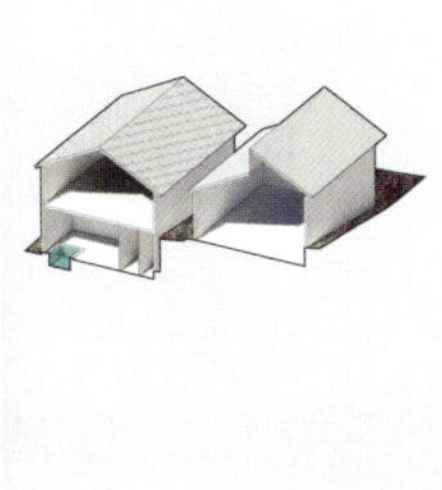

Bibliography

Bernd & Hilla Becher
Jeff L. Rosenheim

Hot Spring Sommelier Textbook
Kazuhiro Toma

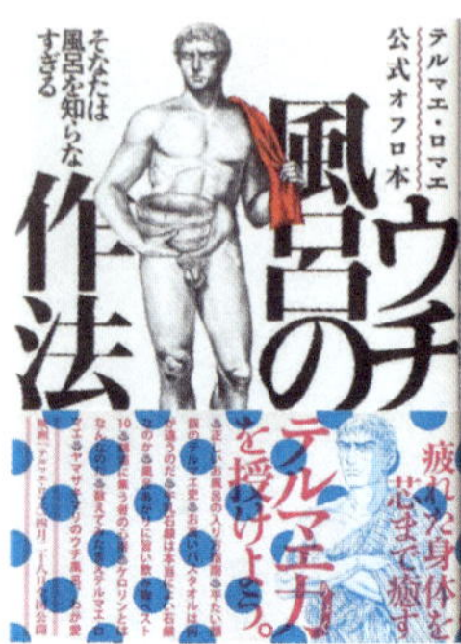

Thermae Romae Bath Book
Kadokawa Publishing

Encyclopedia of Hot Springs in Japan
Fuyuto Noguchi

Towards a New Architecture
Le Corbusier

The History of Hot Springs in Japan
Michio Ishikawa

Architectural Design & Detail #31, Hot Springs and Spas
Architectural Thinking Institute

Sento Certification 1: Learning about Bath Culture from History and Architecture
Machida Shinobu

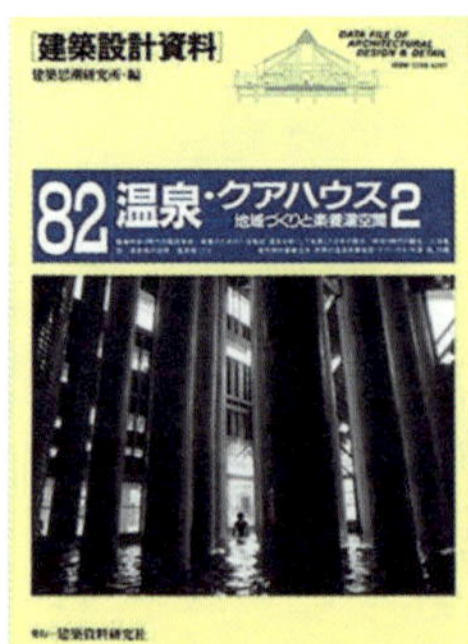

Architectural Design & Detail #82, Hot Springs and Spas 2
Architectural Thinking Institute

Dallol
Jeff Le Cardiet

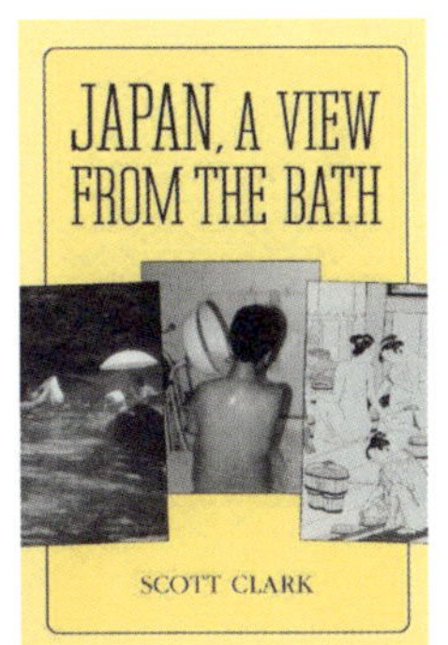

Japan, A View From the Bath
Scott Clark

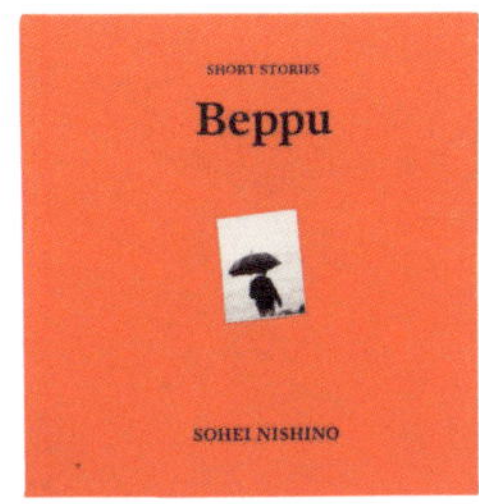

Short Stories: Beppu
Sohei Nishino

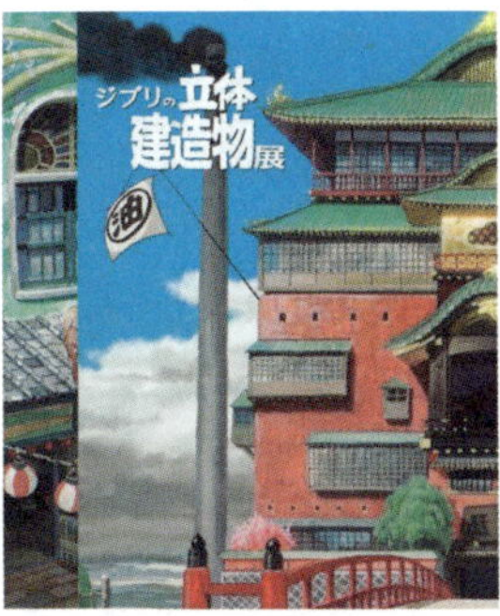

Architecture in Animation
Studio Ghibli

Elements of Architecture
Rem Koolhaas

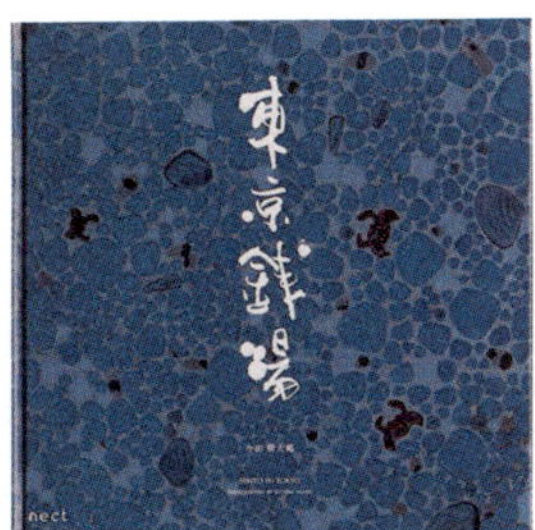

Sento in Tokyo
Kotaro Imada

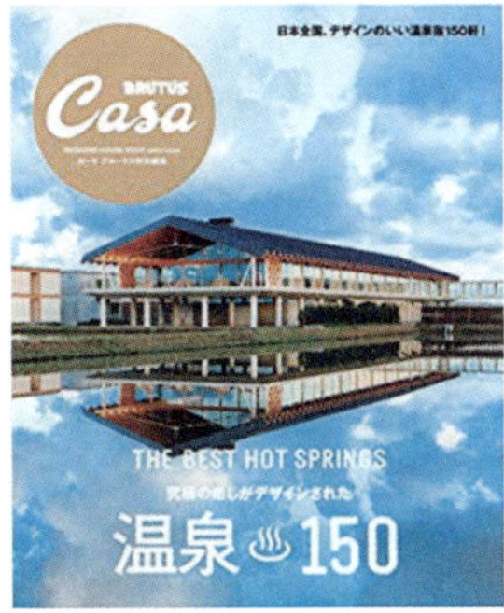

150 Hot Springs
Casa BRUTUS

Sento Certification 2: The Ultimate Bathing Medicine for the Mind and Body
Hayasaka Shinya

The Way of the Japanese Bath
Mark Edward Harris

Further Reading

Masaoka Shiki 正岡子規
– Hateshirazu no ki はて知らずの記
Ozaki Koyo 尾崎紅葉
– Konjikiyasha 金色夜叉
Kyoshi Takahama 高浜虚子
– Iyo no yu 伊予の湯
Wakayama Bokusui 若山牧水
– Minakami kiko みなかみ紀行
– Yamazakura no uta 山桜の歌

THE AUTHOR

Yuval Zohar (湯バル) is an architect and designer working internationally. Born in Israel and raised in the United States, he has spent the majority of his career in Asia.

He currently resides in the small onsen town of Yugawara, in the Japanese countryside.

Credits

Book concept
Yuval Zohar

Texts
Yuval Zohar

Photography
Yuval Zohar, except p. 175: Fireworks / PIXTA, *[Beppu City, Oita Prefecture] Kannawa Onsen town seen from the Yukemuri Observatory*, 2015; p. 177: Daniel Modell, *Midtown Steam Explosion*, 2007; pp. 178–179: Tsubaki Takashi, *Sakurayu* , 2016; p. 202: Jun Liao, *Onsensei*, 2024.

Image Citations
Onsen Artifacts pp. 52–53: kerorin.com, shokunin.com, intojapanwaraku.com, bathclin.co.jp, kao.co.jp, cow-soap.co.jp, dailyportalz.jp/kiji/180319202369, sts.kahaku.go.jp/diversity/document/system/pdf/026_e.pdf, yanagiya-cosme.co.jp/400th/history/section1.html, japan-guide.com/tour/2015/j/south/day9.html, citymilk.net/bin/ote/meiji2.htm, family-chair.co.jp/family-blog/page/8, yanagiya-cosme.co.jp, japanjourneys.jp/kagawa/naoshima/attractions/i-love-yu-bathhouse-sento, kk-sanpoh.co.jp/service_vendor jp.toto.com, inada-massagechair.com/models/dreamwave/index.html, tanaka-scale.co.jp/

Fuji Sento Murals pp. 180–181: allabout-japan.com/en/article/6242/, kt.rim.or.jp/~tsukasa/sento/subete/furoba.htm, fujisancurator.com/blog/2015/12/25/onsen-around-mt-fuji-the-criteria-for-choosing-it, wiki.openstreetmap.org/wiki/File:Mount_Fuji_mural.jpg, kinezuka.jp/kiyotofuji/, mizu111.blog40.fc2.com/blog-entry-605.html, gotokyo.org/en/story/guide/japanese-bathing-culture-uncovered-a-guide-to-sento/index.html, suumo.jp/chintai/bc_100374862537/, kiri-san.com/post/12172, ozmall.co.jp/metromin/article/30449/, tabi-labo.com/309808/wt-mt-fuji-painter-last-challenge

Cover: Tsurunoyu in Nyuto Onsen; inner cover: Sukayu Onsen in Aomori; first spread: Ubayu Onsen in Yamagata.

Drawings
Yuval Zohar

Proof reading
Leo Reijnen

Design
SJG / Joost Grootens, Julie da Silva Lenoir

Printing and lithography
ORO

Publisher
Marcel Witvoet, nai010 publishers

This publication was made possible by financial support from

EXP.

EXP. is an experience platform blending design, art, and technology to craft sustainable ventures that deliver universal human values. Learn more at exp.is

nai010 publishers is an internationally orientated publisher specialized in developing, producing and distributing books in the fields of architecture, urbanism, art and design. www.nai010.com

nai010 books are available internationally at selected bookstores and from the following distribution partners:

North, Central and South America – Artbook | D.A.P., New York, USA, dap@dapinc.com

Rest of the world – Idea Books, Amsterdam, the Netherlands, idea@ideabooks.nl

For general questions, please contact nai010 publishers directly at sales@nai010.com or visit our website www.nai010.com for further information.

ISBN 978-94-6208-880-1
NUR 648
BISAC ARC000000, ARC018000
THEMA AMA